Something After Misfortune

Gabrielle St. Charles

ISBN 1-59109-456-9

Something After Misfortune

Something After Misfortune

To my daughter.

Chapter One

The office was so quiet. I sat at my computer crunching the numbers for the umpteenth time and found no rationale to what the corporate officers said in the meeting. There was no way that this proposal would make $15 million dollars. The closest I could come up with, and that was without marginal error, was an $11.8 million loss.

At a surprise meeting last week, the head of the company asked all the key employees to help finance a business endeavor. We were given this report and told that we would benefit from signing over our retirement funds for five years and in that time, be paid part of the profit from this proposal. The proposal suggested that taking on six new clients from out of country would eventually lead to an overseas expansion. The thought process behind it lacked clarity. For the most part, the clients that they spoke of were getting services similar, nothing unique, in their countries of origin. In order to win the bids, we would have to undercut the pricing, thus losing money. We functioned at just profitability in our bids in the status quo. Everyone else had signed at the meeting, that day, without so much as looking at the numbers.

"Jesus people, this is what we work for daily and they ask us to just toss it away?" I muttered to myself. It frustrated me that it just didn't make sense. I'd been the only person in the room not swayed by their smooth talk and pretty papers. I couldn't do it. I didn't see where they thought this could be profitable, but, then again, I was in the department that handled the actual finances and marketing for the firm. The others weren't privy to information that I was.

To make matters worse, I 'd been pulled into the CEO's office and he warned me that I needed to give them an answer by Monday morning. I knew that if I didn't sign, I'd be terminated. Maybe not today, maybe not tomorrow or the next day, but I'd surely lose my job.

"Shit, shit, shit..." I mumbled to myself. I sat back in my chair and ran my hands through my sandy hair. My head ached, my stomach was in a knot and I felt like someone hit me with a truck. The stress was getting to me. I had no idea what to do. Where would I go from here? I had called my friend, Desiree, and she had advised me to sit tight as long as possible. The owner's of my company did not have the best of reputations.

My thoughts went back to my childhood when we were so poor that my mom couldn't buy our lunches at school. I had sworn to myself then that I'd never have to hurt for money again. I'd done pretty well for myself; coming into the company right out of college, working in the receiving department. I had worked my way up to Senior Executive Marketing Manager, the title I now held. I was hungry in the beginning. I knew I couldn't make partner, because the company was family owned, but I'd done well.

It now seemed it was over. I couldn't release my retirement for this. There was no way that I was going to do this. But, what *would* I do?

My mind was boggled; I ran through every option I might have mentally. I could redirect my IRA. Being a hundred percent vested, it was mine to do with as I pleased. Taking it out early would cost me significantly. I couldn't pay the penalties. The redirection would allow me to stay vested and still contribute. Another option I had was that my boss at the shelter that I volunteered at had offered me a job last week. She'd come in on her night off last weekend and voiced her concern at how I looked so rundown. She questioned if I 'd been eating right and said I looked tired. I explained that I hadn't even been golfing all month and that was unusual. She was probably right; I had looked like hell. The company had been sliding downhill for eight months. The more money they lost, which I couldn't figure out how we were losing money, the more work they required us to do. It just didn't make sense.

It was the first time I'd really talked to her and she drew out of me what was going on here at work. I 'd seen her reaction when I told her; it angered her greatly, a red head for you. Samantha had stood from the table and in her sweet southern drawl had told me in no uncertain terms that if they didn't know what they had, she did. She'd offered me a position right then and there.

At the thought I smiled. I might have to take her up on that offer. My mind flew back to the page in front of me. I liked making this much money, even though I could survive on much less. I 'd become quite accustomed to my lifestyle in the last four years, all but the having to be in the closet. I spent the last seven years working here and hiding my lesbian lifestyle, living in some sort of darkness.

My phone rang and brought me out of my thoughts rapidly. I jumped at the sound. Who could be calling me at this hour? It was one o'clock in the morning. The switchboard was off and the only way to get through was this line. No one had the direct line number. I gave it to no one but family.

"Hello?" I answered, my disgust with the numbers subsiding when I heard Samantha's silky voice on the other end of the line.

"Abigail?" She sounded as startled as I was.

"Hi, Sam. How are you?" I said.

"Good, really good. I..." she stammered a little before she continued, "I hope you don't mind me calling you so late. You aren't upset are you?"

I found myself laughing softly and said, "I don't mind at all. What's up?"

I reclined back in my chair, enjoying the softness of her voice and the gentle manner in which she explained how she and been thinking about me, and my predicament. She then spoke of nonsense things at the center, told me about her day of disaster that day and for the next few moments she literally relaxed me to the point that I began to yawn.

"I'm sorry about that. I didn't mean to yawn on you." I apologized.

"Oh, don't worry about it. I know you've been exhausted. It's late..." There was a long silence before she spoke again. Out of the blue, she asked, "What are you doing after you leave the office?

Caught of guard, I replied, "Well, I hadn't really thought about it. I usually just go home." I figured they needed me at the shelter. "I could come in if you need me?"

She laughed softly again, something I found very appealing, her laughter. "Have you eaten, Abby?" She spoke so softly I could barely hear her.

"No," my voice matched hers. I was embarrassed. I hadn't had time. "I had a meeting over lunch with the corporate officers, I missed dinner and well, I just didn't have time. I forgot."

"Wanna stop by my place on your way home?" There was no sound on the other side of the line. The silence was very noticeable.

Samantha was such a caring soul. She'd been worried about me and now she was going to take care of me.

She spoke again, her sultry voice very low and very smoky. "I could feed you."

I was the one laughing now. Realizing that my stomach was past the point of growling in hunger, "Okay. But, are you sure? I could stop by the diner; it's only a block from my house. I don't want to be any trouble; I don't want to intrude."

She refused to listen to that. "How much longer are you going to be? I made some pasta this evening and have plenty left. I could heat it up with no trouble whatsoever. I wouldn't mind sharing it with you."

It did sound inviting and I was starving. "All I have to do is get my desk back in order and I am ready to leave."

I jotted down her address and noted that it was very near

my home. I politely accepted her invitation once again and told her I would be there in twenty to thirty minutes.

"Good. It's a plan then. I'll see you in a bit." She sounded excited as she hung up the phone.

Chapter Two

I sat there with my phone still in my hand, and found myself smiling. I had no idea why this woman had taken it upon herself to be my friend; I rarely opened up to anyone anymore. I'd been out of a relationship for over two years, hadn't even dated this time. My last relationship ended very badly and very abruptly. I thought it would last forever and it had ended with my lover cheating on me the entire last year of our relationship. I found her in bed with one of my friends one night. I'd come home early from a conference on our anniversary to surprise her. I had flowers and a beautiful necklace wrapped in pretty paper.

It still amazed me; but it didn't hurt any longer. I always told myself that; tried to convince myself it didn't hurt. But, in reality, it only stopped hurting, because I stopped caring if I were ever with anyone again.

That relationship had lasted four years. With it ending so badly, I 'd lost my faith in not only others, but I'd lost my faith in myself. How could I have been so ignorant? I didn't even know. I really walked in that night, completely ignorant. I was almost to the bed, stumbled on them, and I still didn't see it. Even when I saw it, I didn't really see it. I saw the back of my best friends head. I recognized her right off. And silly me; wondered what she and her girlfriend were doing at my house.

As I sat there thinking the phone started beeping that annoying beep and saying, "If you would like to make a call, hang up and dial again." It brought me back to the office.

I was still sitting there holding the phone in my hand, my chin in my other hand, leaning on my desk. What a sight I must be? Why was I thinking about that? Samantha wasn't a lesbian. Here I was thinking back to long lost love. I must make an appointment on Monday to see someone about my mental health.

" I've lost it." I giggled.

As I straightened my office up and put the papers I had been working on in my computer case I found my thoughts wandering back to Samantha. She had the softest auburn hair that bounced off her shoulders. It was wavy, but not really curly. I often found myself wanting to reach out and wrap a wave around my finger. She had soft greenish blue eyes that were striking against her dark lashes. I had noticed myself getting lost in them when she was talking to me.

She was such a good listener. I'd told her so much about myself in such a short period of time. I'd even mentioned my last relationship, and to a straight woman at that. I found she gave me what seemed to be an honest opinion and I appreciated that.

As I cleaned up the rest of my things, grabbed my computer case and my purse, and put back on my navy heels, I kept thinking about Samantha's lips. Maybe I shouldn't go to her house? Something was wrong with me. I was finding myself attracted to this woman and that was *not* good news. I hadn't been attracted to someone in a long time and it wasn't like me to be attracted to straight women. Maybe I did need therapy?

The walk to the elevator was dark and quiet. An eerie silence fell over the offices at night. The security guard knew I was there; he'd stopped by several times to make sure I was okay during the course of the night. He'd even brought me a bottle of Evian, made light conversation, and I was thankful to know that he was there. As I headed down in the elevator, I thought again about Samantha and how soft she looked the night we had talked six days ago. We had spoken on Saturday night until the wee hours of the morning. It had ended with a crisis call I had to take and she'd left me a note telling me that if I ever needed to talk again to give her a call and had left her number.

I had 't wanted to intrude and considering my hectic work schedule, had spent most of my evenings in the office that week, trying to decide what I would do. Thinking back, I had no recollection of where I had even put her number. She was so soft. Her manner of speaking and her look were so classy. She was definitely beautiful. She had very cute glasses, I thought as I noticed myself smiling as I leaned against the elevator walls. The bell dinged, breaking my thoughts and I walked out of the elevator to find my little security guard friend there. I jumped; startled that he was right there as the door opened.

We both had a nervous laugh as we said goodnights to each other. He was just as shocked as I was.

I hated to walk outside by myself, to walk across the street to the parking lot where we all parked; it sort of spooked me when it was late. At least it wasn't far, but a lone woman was never a good thing at night. I had learned just how rough the city was on the crisis calls I took at the domestic violence shelter. I'd walked out many a night with my mace in my hand, but still felt unprotected.

I was getting nervous about seeing Samantha again. Why did she want me to come over? Maybe she wanted to offer me the job again. That was it. I was good at what I did. The Center had an appropriation given to them two weeks ago and Samantha, in charge of hiring, had not found the right person for this position. The position would work along side Samantha's position, and maybe that was something I would have to think about also. I didn't think being attracted to her was a good idea at this point. Oh, great, what was I going to do? I needed a friend badly right now and she was a great friend, I could tell by how the other women at the shelter respected her.

She worked statewide in her field and helped many women in crisis. That was it!!! I was a woman in crisis and she just wanted to help me. For the first time in a long time, I decided I could use it and I would let her help me. And, there was nothing more to it; she knew I needed help and she was going to be there for me. I would make a new friend. That wasn't such a bad thought.

And, I guess I would just have to get over this little crush I was beginning to have on little miss Samantha.

I drove to Samantha's with no real thoughts, just music from the radio. The strings soothing my soul as I drove. I would begin looking for work on Monday. I could not give the retirement fund to the company. I had worked too hard for what I had and I could roll it over into an IRA. That was what I would do. Tonight over this late dinner, I would speak to Samantha about that position. Maybe it would be a good thing. I wouldn't have to be in the closet and I could use my marketing skills to actually benefit someone who needed it. The money really didn't matter. I would probably like the position.

I was convincing myself. That's what I would do, I thought, as I pulled into her driveway. It really wasn't that far away, I noticed as I shut my car off. She had a great lawn, very well taken care of just as she was. There were flowers across the front of the porch, which wrapped around the back of the house, as did the porch. The porch was screened in and had furniture arranged as if it were prepared for a tea party, so quaint and demure. There was one light on in the house, the living room it seemed.

My hands were sweating and my heart was pounding, as I walked up the three wooden stairs and entered the screened porch. It smelled like potpourri, apple and cinnamon. I took a deep breath and knocked lightly on the door.

It was only seconds before she answered. Such a quick response startled me a bit, but she was so friendly with her smile as she opened the door wide for me to come on in, that made me feel a bit more at ease. I entered her house and felt immediately at home. The furniture was right out of a Country Collection. It was fabulous, rustic yet modern. The colors were navy and forest, highlighted with peach accents. It fit my taste to a tee, warm and inviting.

The light was dim and the scent of berries, a mix of the candles she had lit all over and the potpourri baskets scattered on end tables, tantalized my senses. It was beautiful. She closed the door and touched my shoulder, which made me shiver as she motioned to take my coat and she said hello. I let my coat fall over my shoulders into her hands, she took it and tossed it over the back of an antique arm chair that sat alone in the corner with a reading lap and rustic table.

"I'm glad you came," she said.

This was a great house. There was a bookcase along the south wall that filled the entire wall space. It had books in every nook and cranny. She must be well versed. I liked that. I turned to look at her and to say thank you but she was walking away from me into the other room.

This room was dimly lit also, almost dark, but I followed her. She walked through that room, what must be another living room, back into a dining area. As I entered the doorway to the dining area, I was in utter amazement. The room looked like it came out of a magazine. It had a cherry table, six chairs, and a candelabrum, with peach candles, seven of them. It had peach and forest place mats, which were set with service for two. The candles were all that lit the room.

The food smelled wonderful, baked manicotti with marinara and steamed veggies. The settings were right together, not at the end of the table, we would be setting right next to each other. The hair on the back of my neck stood straight up.

All the sudden I missed my long hair. I'd gotten a new style about six months ago, one that was cut just at my earlobes. I liked it and it was easier to handle, but I was now cold, the chill running all the way through my body.

She turned around and faced me for the first time. I had stopped dead in my tracks following her and she was a couple of feet in front of me, near the table.

She asked me, "What's the matter?"

Okay, what do I say to that? I have no idea, I am in a straight woman's home; attracted to her; I feel as if I walked into my dream home; it smells so good and I am starving and I could not possibly eat if I had to sit that close to her; she smells wonderful and she is gorgeous. What could I reply to that?

As I stood there and thought about it, I had no answer. She moved closer to me, which caused me to back up a step and she looked at me with a grin, a twinkle in her eye. She kept walking toward me, each step closer making me more and more nervous. There was nowhere to run. What was she doing? Oh, God, was I tired.

She was directly in front of me, looking me eye-to-eye, the best she could, she was a good seven inches shorter than I. My 5'11" seemed to be an advantage at this point, especially to her possible 5'4" at the most. She was close enough to me that I could barely breathe, the cold doorway stopping my movement backwards. Even though I was afraid, I tried to fake security of self.

I looked into her eyes, but made no reply and no move. I felt out of sorts in my navy business suit. My hose were choking me and my white polo needed the top button undone under my jacket. Why was I so uncomfortable?

She was so close, I could feel her breath on my skin; she was directly in front of me as she spoke to me. Everything was racing, my pulse, my mind, and my nerves.

"You look terrified? Am I making you nervous?" She didn't break eye contact.

All I could get out was a muttered, "Yes, you are."

My heart was pounding, my hands were making puddles on the floor; I was sure. I had sweat dripping down between my breasts. It was hot in here. She didn't move. Not one iota, not one muscle. She didn't move. Why was I here? This was a huge mistake. What did she want from me?

All the sudden I felt the demand of desire, something I had not felt for so long. She was so close that when I breathed in, her perfume, faint and crisp, invaded my senses. She just stood there looking at me.

I must have looked frantic at that point. She reached her right hand up to my shoulder as she tipped up on her toes. I felt her move closer to my face as I closed my eyes. Oh My God!

What was going on? Her lips touched mine just briefly. I was frozen. She just kissed me? And then she was gone. When I opened my eyes, she was walking away. She pulled out a chair to the table and motioned me to come sit down. How my legs got me there, I have no idea. But I sat down.

She moved behind me and reached down in front of me. Her hands slid down my shoulders, over my breasts softly to the buttons on my jacket. The big brass buttons were opened immediately and she had my jacket off my shoulders and arms. She moved to hang my jacket on the chair at the end of the table, next to me. I still had no perception of what was going on. She moved back behind me and leaned down a bit, her hands back on my shoulders, massaging gently.

"Is this okay?" she asked.

 I nodded my head as I closed my eyes. It had been such an incredibly long time since a woman had touched me in this manner, a very long time.

She spoke again into my ear, "I wanted to kiss you last Saturday night, when you talked to me. I haven't stopped thinking about you since that night. I made myself leave when you got that call, so that nothing inappropriate happened at the shelter. I was afraid of what I might do."   Her voice was husky now, very passionate and soft. It was seductive, as was her house, this setting, and the table.

The foods smell wafted up, my stomach caught it and growled.

"You're hungry, aren't you?" She moved around to the side, between the chair I was sitting on and her chair. Her leg slid over mine and she straddled me, my hands instinctively went to her outer thighs to help her. It was a tight fit between the table, and us even though she was petite.

She took my face in her hands and lifted it to her. "Are you okay with all this? You haven't said a thing"

For the first time, she looked as if she had lost her confidence. I knew nothing about her, but apparently she wasn't as straight as I thought she was.

I was starting to get my wits about me, finally, and nodded

yes. It was fine. She kissed me again, this time I responded to her kiss. Her lips softly brushed against mine, as if to tease me into responding. She didn't know she needed no help. Her tongue gently traced the line of my lips as I reached toward her with my lips to kiss her fully. My hands moved to her back to pull her closer to me. She was almost the same height as I was with us sitting down, my long legs holding most of my height.

Her arms went around my shoulders, leaving my face where they had warmed me, and she embraced me so gently. She kissed me with as much class as she evaded. Her lips were soft and full, demanding but not rough in any way. Her tongue gently prodded my tongue to respond to her. My lips brushed hers, gently following her lead. It was very natural. It felt as if my lips belonged to her. She had me responding to her fully.

As if on cue, that she had me where she wanted me, she pulled her lips from mine and took her arms from around my shoulders. She pulled back as she opened her eyes and reached around to the plate behind her. I watched diligently.

She cut the food with perfection, her hands graceful and smooth. She laid down the fork and knife and picked up a piece of manicotti. She brought it to my lips and I welcomed it. The moment it hit my tongue, I could taste the perfection with which she seasoned it. She kissed my lips as I chewed the delightful tidbit.

"I told you I wanted to feed you tonight," she said with a grin.

Her eyes glistened as she said it, with a devilish tinge. She was wicked, I could tell. She was not just classy, but had a side to her that I bet one rarely saw. This was nothing like the woman who was so comforting to me last week, but I wasn't complaining.

She reached for a bite of veggies and fed me again. This time kissing my cheek to my earlobe while I chewed. She couldn't possibly know what she was doing to me as she fed me, bite after bite, paying homage to my neck, ear and lips while I ate. Before I knew it, the food on my plate was gone, and she looked at me quizzically.

"What would you like now?"

But, before I could answer, she removed herself from my lap and walked into the other room. I was left there, sitting alone.

In the other room, I heard music come on, my favorite classical piece. She couldn't have known my tastes that well? It was playing loud enough I could hear it clearly, but I could tell she was rooms from me. It was a good five minutes before she appeared in the door way again. For the first time, I noticed what she was wearing. She had on Levi button up jeans, a navy sweater with cream trim and lots of gold. Almost every finger had a ring on it, even her right thumb. I had noticed that the night before, when we had talked. She leaned against the doorway and brought her right hand up and motioned with her finger for me to come to her, and she turned around and left again.

This was great! I had no idea what was going on, but it was great. I had no intentions of sleeping with this woman, none whatsoever. I knew that I had such willpower that I would hold onto that, no matter what she did tonight...no matter how badly I hurt between my legs at that point...

I got up from the chair and moved into the other room, leaving my heels behind by my chair. I walked through the hallway; on the left was the kitchen, large and immaculate. On the right, in the first doorway, it looked to be a guest room, the bed turned down. That was all I could see from the light coming in the window. The next room on the right was an office. And there was one final room on each side.

The right showed another bedroom, it was dark and I couldn't see much, but there was a light on in the room on the left, the door open only a few inches. She heard me, because the door opened and there she was again. I could see behind her, she had run a bath, there were candles lit along the sunken tub; the music was coming from in here. It looked inviting, but there was no way I was taking a bath with this woman. No way!

She looked at me...as I looked at the bubble bath that was run, and she smiled again.

"You can get undressed when I leave, it's for you. I will be out here reading when you're done. Take as long as you like." And, with that, she walked away. She left me standing once again.

I entered the bathroom and looked around. It was huge. There was a vanity inside, with various makeup accessories, curling iron, hair dryer, etc. And another bookshelf, this one smaller but with wonderful titles tucked in the corner. I guess that the bath looked inviting enough to go for it, because I undressed and slid right in. I loved to bath, and I wasn't hungry anymore, and well, Samantha knew how to do it up right.

The music was soft and sensuous and the bath was warm. As I slid into it, I could feel the tension in my body. She had me more tense than work. I laid my head back onto a bath pillow and kicked my feet up on the opposite end. I wondered to myself why they made tubs without making them long enough for tall people. I closed my eyes and began to relax.

There was a soft knock at the door, the knock made me realize I was naked in another woman's house, in her bath to boot. What an idiot I was.

"Can I come in?" she asked.

What was I going to say? If she was naked, I would just get out of the bath, put my clothes on and leave. It was that simple. I had respected her when she left me alone to bath. But now, here she was again. I was not sure what to do. I still knew virtually nothing about this woman. I was a fool...naked and bare in her bath.

"Yes." I heard myself betray me and say.

I kept my eyes closed as she entered. When I felt her move to the tub and kneel down on the soft peach rug, I opened my eyes, to see if I needed to get out and go home. Was I going to find a naked woman? There she was, in her classy demure way, once again brilliant. She had not removed a piece of clothing, but had brought me dessert.

What a charmer she was. All of the sudden very self-conscious, I looked down to make sure that nothing was showing under the bubbles, and was nicely surprised to see that I was fully covered. She had a tray with her, and she sat it down on the stand next to the tub. The tub was sunken, but you had to climb two steps to get to it. She'd knelt down on the floor just below the steps, but now moved so that she was sitting on the top step, her tray within reach.

On it sat a bowl of strawberries and cherries, a bowl of brown sugar, and a bowl of what looked like yogurt or sour cream. She smiled slyly at me again, reached for a strawberry and dipped it in the white cream and then the brown sugar. She brought it to my lips as they parted to accept it. I took a bite of the strawberry. It was amazing. It was sour cream, but the brown sugar covered any bitterness or sour taste in it.

She dipped about five of the strawberries and cherries, alternating between feeding me and eating them alone, licking her fingers after she fed me mine. I didn't know if they were actually good, or if it was that she fed them to me that made them so wonderfully delicious.

"Is the water cooling too much?" she asked.

"No, it's fine, thank you." I had never spent this much time with someone and really not found out anything about her. We had never talked about her; I now wanted to know about her.

"Why are you doing this for me?" I asked.

She dipped another strawberry, very deliberately this time, and leaned forward and kissed me before she ate it herself, a soft kiss.

"I like you." She kept doing what she was doing, paying no never-mind to me.

Okay, that was a big bomb. I got nowhere with that question.

She spoke slowly, her eyes penetrating, "I like you and I want to get to know you. You're so independent." She paused and readjusted herself. "You've worked at the shelter for over two years, and no one knows anything about you, but where you work. I want to know more."

With that, she kissed me again, this time her hand sliding under the water to my left breast and as she kissed me, she caressed my breast. I moaned gently. I definitely felt the underdog here. I kissed her back, never exceeding the limits of her kiss, but letting her lead completely. She kissed me for a bit and then removed her hand. She grabbed a hand towel from the rack and stood up. Her movement made enough of the air stir to make me chill, she saw me shudder.

"You're cold. Here, I'll lay this towel here and you can dry off, would you like something to wear, a little more comfy?"

The thought of putting my suit back on did not appeal to me. But why was this woman doing this, and what did she expect? She had fed me, which was what she had said she wanted to do. I didn't know how to answer. She left the room without me saying anything. She returned immediately with a pair of flannel sleeping pants, a big sweatshirt, and a pair of white socks.

"Thank you, Samantha. I really appreciate it. You are kind beyond measure." I stammered. With a nervous smile I said, "Thank you."

She nodded and left the room, leaving me alone again.

I had mixed feelings this time. If I put on these nice, warm, inviting clothes, what was next? She couldn't have any other plans. Was I to go home in socks and no shoes? I had nothing to wear on my feet. Or, was she intending to seduce me? I was not going to be seduced tonight. Not by someone I barely knew and worked with at that. Okay, I shook my head a little. I was too tired to think about it. I knew she had a guest room. I could stay there if I had to...I was sure at this point, she wouldn't do more than kick me out and if she didn't do that, I would curl up in her guest room or drive the short way home with no shoes on.

I put on the flannels. They fit perfectly. They were long enough, so apparently they were not hers. The sweatshirt was just right too. I looked at the size before I put it on. It was an XL; she would have swum in it. Oh well, she had a past, we all did. I put it all on, pulled on the socks and felt right at home. I let the bath out, rinsed the tub, looked at my hair and makeup and was mortified. I looked a mess. I ran my hands through my hair. I had gotten it a little wet in the tub, so it went back into shape pretty easily. If I could get to my purse, I could put a little eye-makeup on, but as it was, I just had the mascara left from this morning. It was going to have to be enough. I pinched my cheeks a little to give them more color and ran my fingers over my lips to make them redder. There, that was going to have to be good enough.

Here I go again, what am I doing? I do not want to go here, but then again, I might want to one day and must do the best I can to preserve my image, even the one of the ice princess that I carried around so well the last couple of years. One last look in the mirror and out I went.

As I entered the hallway, I looked in each room, not knowing where I would find Samantha, but ready for a surprise again. This woman had more up her sleeve; I just knew it. I got all the way back to the dining room to find it was clean, not a trace of us having been in there. I went back past the second living room; she wasn't in there, to the first room I had come into. There she was, reading, sitting on a couch, all curled up in a quilt.

I hadn't noticed the fireplace before, but she had a crackling fire burning. The room was warm and sedate. She had the stereo playing softly, I didn't recognize the music, but it was classical and very nice. She looked up at me when I came in and put her book away.

"Did you have a nice bath?" she inquired.

"Yes, very nice, thank you."

She got up and came over to me again, within inches of my face. "What would you like to do now?"

I had no idea, why was she doing this to me. I couldn't

think straight, let alone make a decision, and she was standing so close again. She took my hands in hers, both of them and led me to the couch.

"Would you like to sit and talk?"

I could handle that, "Yes, that would be nice."

There were a lot of questions I wanted to ask her. She definitely intrigued me. She sat down on the couch and when I tried to sit a little bit away from her, she pulled on my hand and brought me right next to her.

"I make you nervous, don't I?" She was laughing softly.

I had to be honest, "Yeah, a little, I am not used to this, it's been a long time. And I thought you were straight." I said with a little laugh.

"Well, you were assuming, weren't you? I was in a relationship for the last eleven years, with a woman. We split up two years ago and I haven't dated since." She was brushing my hand with her finger gently stirring up sensation.

"You sound like me. I haven't dated either. I haven't really thought much about it. I figured if I worked hard enough, I wouldn't have to think about it."

She then did something that charmed me even more. She laid her head up against my shoulder and snuggled really close to me.

"Can I tell you about my life?" She asked.

"I would like that." I put my arms around her loosely. I was still very uncomfortable in the most comfortable of ways.

She then told me all about her relationship. That she had grown up in North Carolina, and been with her partner there for eleven years. She slowly explained that she had thought that it was forever, but her partner had come to her one day and said she wanted out. It had devastated her. I could feel the tears begin to seep through my sweatshirt as she continued her story. I stroked her hair, laid my head on hers and held her as she spoke softly, with love, about her former partner. I could hear the southern accent the more she talked. She must be getting tired, I thought. She nuzzled even more closely after she finished talking.

She had told me that after they split up, she left her position in North Carolina and moved here. She intended to start completely over. She and her partner had purchased a home together; her partner had kept it for a few months and then sold it and given her half. To help herself feel more comfortable, she sold her car, one that matched Lauren's, and bought a Rodeo. She had attempted to change her whole life. She felt as if she didn't ever want to be in a relationship again, and had kept the vow to herself until she had met me. Saying that, she snuggled close and I could hear her weeping softly.

As strange as it was to hear her talk about me that way, it was comfortable as well. We had worked together for over a year and I knew her, I just didn't 'know' her. I kissed her head. I kissed her for all the compassion she gave me the week before, for all the "together" she alluded to, and for the pain I heard her express. I felt very special that she had chosen me to open up to.

"Are you okay, Samantha? I don't mean this moment, I mean are you really okay now?"

She pulled back out of my arms and moved to where she could look at me again. She took her fingers and moved my hair behind my ears, something I did often, and then she kissed me lightly. She brushed her lips so tenderly against mine. Her hands still holding my face, she cradled me softly with her kiss and her hands. She was so gentle. She was so soft and yet so tough.

I had seen her take a man down to nothing in a second flat. I had admired her expertise in the field. When a crisis came in, she took over with a confidence that would amaze man, woman or child. She handled situations daily that were traumatic for all involved. We saw women beaten and bruised, near death at times and whole families torn apart by abuse or neglect. We saw men beat women to a pulp for nothing more than control, or a woman in the shelter, shunned by family and friends for being raped. We saw it all, and I had seen Samantha deal with these things like no one else. And here the woman, whom I respected so much for her confidence and strength, was crying in my arms.

I began to take control of the kiss; I explored her lips and made her move her body closer to mine with my passion. She began to respond to my probing. I could feel her giving me control, but she definitely met my passion. She was a great kisser. I could always tell from the first kiss what kind of relationship I would have with a woman, or at least potential relationship. This would be a good one.

We kissed for a long time. Never wanting to stop, I kept kissing her, deeper sometimes, and softer at others. Letting the emotion ebb and flow with the kissing. She caressed me as I caressed her, always over the clothing and not provocatively. It was very comfortable. I got the feeling she was not just in this for sex and that made me feel so much better. I could relax and express whatever it was I was beginning to feel for her.

Samantha pulled back her lips from mine after kissing me so deeply she nearly made me cry. The kiss was so passionate, her body thrown against mine, finally. I wanted her, and bad. But this was completely out of character for me. I never got intimate without knowing the woman well. My hands were holding her as close to me as I could get her. I wanted to make love with her. But, I still had my wits about me enough to know that I knew too little.

I moved away, reluctantly, as she pulled her lips from mine, to look at her. It had to be late. The night had been so moving that I had no idea what time it possibly was, and I didn't care. She looked up at me, "Do you have to work tomorrow?"

Luckily, I didn't. It was Saturday and I didn't have to go into the office and I wasn't volunteering this weekend at the shelter, so I was free. "No, I don't. I am completely free. Why?"

It was nice to just settle back with her. She fell into my arms once again, and we just lay on the couch. As we had kissed, we lost altitude and were more lying at this point. She fit in my arms perfectly.

"What did you expect tonight?" she asked me.

She had this way of asking me things and then caressing me and kissing me where I could barely answer her.

"I had expected to come over and have more of the same thing we had at the shelter last weekend. That I had noticed how beautiful you were last weekend; for the first time really being around you. I had seen you at work with others, but never really paid attention to you until last weekend when we were talking." I also said, "I expected a straight woman attempting to get me to work for the shelter full time."

She laughed at me. She literally giggled at my words. I got up, moved to a position where I could straddle her and hold her down.

"What are you laughing at?" I said as I laughed too. "I really thought you were straight."

She just laughed harder. Her eyes were watering she was laughing so hard now.

"I can't believe you're laughing at me. I pour my heart out to you and you are laughing." I faked being hurt. "Oh great! I am never telling you anything again."

She was laughing so hard; I could barely sit on her. She was moving about, trying to get me off her. I took a hold of her wrists as she begged for mercy. But, I wouldn't give in.

"OKAY, OKAY...I give up...You win. I am laughing at the thought of myself being straight." She calmed a little and her voice went back to the sexy southern drawl. "That is hilarious to me. I have wanted you from the first day I saw you walk into the shelter. It's been no secret to my staff. They've begged me to ask you out. All along, I am thinking your ice princess status is quite right. I couldn't get near you. I tried. Do you realize how many times I have called you into the shelter on those nights to take calls, feeling so guilty, because I knew you had another job, but wanted to talk to you?" she was serious now. "You would come in and disappear. I would find you in the crisis phone room, reading or doing paperwork alone. My plans backfired so often."

I was amazed. She *had* called me in a number of times to take calls on nights I never even got a call. Nights that were fully staffed. So, I would just sit in the room alone and do work to keep my mind off things. I loved being there; at least I had company, the sound of people, instead of at my house, where there was no one but the cat and myself. It was comforting for me being at the shelter. And all along she wanted to talk to me? I leaned down and kissed her.

She had started calling me last year. Oh, she couldn't have wanted me that long, poor thing. I felt so guilty. I hadn't even noticed her, until the other night. I had thought of her briefly throughout the week, but mostly about the job she had offered me, not allowing myself to think of her beauty. I ran my tongue across her lips passionately, and pressed my body to hers as I laid myself on top of her, spreading her legs with one of mine as I placed it between hers. She was right there with me. Her legs wrapped around mine and she pressed against me from below as she kissed me back. Her hands slid up my sweatshirt to my back. Her nails dug into my skin as I kissed her harder. She moaned loudly as I moved my thigh so that it touched her and she arched to meet me.

The next thing I knew, we were on the floor and she was on top of me. Somehow she rolled us off the couch onto the floor. She was over me that wicked look again in her eyes. I gasped at the sight of her beauty.

"Not so fast Ice Princess." she said.

I just gazed into her eyes. She was truly beautiful. She moved so that she was sitting on my hips. I could feel how wet I had become. She was intriguing. I had no idea what to expect from her, but was beginning to enjoy that. I had trusted her at the shelter and for some reason I trusted her now.

It must have taken the fun out of it for her, because the next thing she said was, "You aren't scared of me anymore, are you?"

I replied easily this time, "No, I'm not."

"Good." she said, "because I don't want you to ever be afraid of me."

I knew I was stronger than she was, so I pushed myself up to sitting. I was now sitting with her still on my thighs, and we kissed again. This time the kiss was soft and sweet, no demands. I ran my fingers through her hair as we kissed and she pulled me closer to her. And then we held each other. The music had stopped and the fire was nearly out, I laid my head on her shoulder.

"I am not afraid of you, and I don't even know you."

She replied to me softly, "I know, but I want to know you. I want to be able to make love to you, to know you inside and out. I want to be a part of you."

That moved me. I had always looked at potential relationships beyond the sexual nature. And it seemed as if she did too.

"Do you want to make love to me now?" I said.

"Oh yes, I would love to, but I won't. If you were that type of person, you would have never let me leave the bath with you tonight. I have taken my cues from you. I saw the look of fear in your eyes when you thought you would find me in there, already in the bath or something. I don't ever want you to fear me. I tried to gain your trust tonight. And I did, didn't I?"

She had. She had done the most important thing; she had let me move at my pace. I knew that at this point, it seemed that she and I had gone pretty fast, but it didn't feel that way. I looked into her eyes once again and I knew she felt my trust.

She kissed me quickly and got to her feet, gave me her hand and helped me to mine. She then walked to the fireplace, myself in tow, and put out the rest of the fire.

Chapter Three

After the fire was out, she led me to her bedroom, walking down
the hall backwards, very slowly, as if to make sure that I would
be willing to follow. I was willing, because I trusted her to just
sleep, to kiss and to hold me, as I wanted to do to her. I followed
without hesitation.

She drew me in to her lair, classy and demure. To my
surprise, her bed was huge. She backed right into it and fell, as
she hit it she pulled me on top of her. I was half-standing but
laying also. I kissed her when we landed. After that, we scooted
to the top of the bed, pulled the covers down and slid under the
sheets together. The pillows were fluffy and soft and I sank into
one as she crushed my lips with hers. This time there was no
hesitation at all; she climbed onto me and parted my legs with
hers. She moved her hips on mine driving me wild. I moaned
without shame. I wanted her so badly. My hands slid up under
her shirt and sweater, over her stomach slowly, to just below her
breast. I stopped there and pulled my lips from hers. I leaned
as far into the pillow as I could, so that I could see her eyes, as
I slid my hand to her breast and took her nipple in between my
fingers. She closed her eyes and moaned.

That night, I explored Samantha's body as she did mine,
without ever taking a piece of clothing off. I felt closer to her
than I had felt to anyone else before. I felt the way she touched
me: lovingly, passionately, and with tenderness. I touched her in
the same manner.

I was so tired, that while we were lying there, as she was
kissing my neck, I whispered to her, "Honey, I have no energy
left; I can't stay awake."

"Let me kiss you to sleep…just drop off whenever you need to, I understand." she whispered back.

And, I did. I slept in her arms that night. I was secure, comfortable and safe.

I awoke the next morning at eleven forty-five. The sun was shining in through the window blinds. I felt so refreshed and with a sigh of contentment, I rolled over to find Samantha, but she was gone. As I leaned up to look over the bed, I saw a note on her pillow.

The note read, "*Darling, I had to run a couple of errands. Last night was the most beautiful night I've ever experienced. I hope you're still here when I get home. I'll be back around 4 PM. If you aren't, I understand. If you don't have plans, I would like to share tonight with you also. I had to run by work and do some quick things and then pick up some things from the store. I hope to see you tonight. Fondly, Sam.*"

I read the note and thought to myself, this is one woman I am going to love getting to know. I was definitely going to be back for this evening. I made a mental note of what I had to do in order to free myself up. I had to break plans and get some things and I wanted to shower and refresh, so I got up from the bed all the while thinking of her touch and having little tummy tugs run through my body.

I looked in her nightstand, hoping to find paper and a pen without finding anything else, and did. I wrote her a note back.

My note said, "*Dearest Sam, I would enjoy sharing your evening with you. I went home to get a shower, freshen up and grab some things myself. If you beat me back, which I hope you do, because I don't want to sit on your porch for all the neighbors to stare at…. Then know that I am awaiting the next chance to kiss your sweet lips and to gaze into your eyes so that I feel as though I did last night. I thought it was beautiful too. Thank You, Sam.*" And, I signed my name.

With that, I gathered my clothing from the bathroom, she had hung it all up and placed my shoes with it. I turned to find that she had written on the bathroom mirror in lipstick, "You are the greatest kisser!!!" I giggled out loud.

I went to the living room, walking on air, where I found a basket of fresh bagels, some juice and directions to the kitchen on another note. I really liked this woman. I grabbed a bagel and the glass of juice and out the door I went.

The drive home was uneventful. My cat, however, was furious upon my arrival. She ignored me when I walked in, but was quick to run when I opened her food and fed her. I played my messages to find the one from Samantha. It said something about calling me at work; she hoped that I was okay, but that she thought they might need help at the shelter. I laughed as I thought about it; she was trying her old ploy to get me to work again last night. I wondered what spurred her to call me so late at work? I made a mental note; I would have to ask her about that tonight.

I jumped in the shower. It felt so good to let the hot water run over my body. My body ached from the night before; I had not used these muscles in years. I hadn't had someone else's weight on me for quite some time. A bit of panic ran through me, what if I couldn't remember how to make love? It had been two years. I had slept with only one person since my breakup and it was terrible. I had stopped halfway through, telling her I couldn't do this, because she was my friend. I had almost lost her friendship. That night of horror began with her trying to console me, we'd been drinking wine, and I found out just how human I was. It was a mess. Well, I couldn't do anything but try. Maybe Samantha would understand. It was too late to worry about it, because last night was so special. It was well worth a try.

After I showered, I sat down and looked at my mail. There wasn't anything particularly interesting, so I tossed it aside.

"Now for some planning for the evening." I got a pen and paper out and made a list. After that, I went and got dressed.

I dressed in a white tee, the sexiest panty-bra set I had and white socks. I then put on dark Levi's and a navy polo oxford. I grabbed my brown and forest Sporto boots and then headed for my jewelry box. I accented with gold hoop ear rings, my gold Gucci watch, a gold chain that held my favorite gold medallion and four rings, all gold but one silver thumb ring. I sprayed my favorite perfume, Tommy Girl, it was crisp and clean and fit what I had in mind. I packed a bag for the night and some clothes for tomorrow, just in case. I then did my hair and put on my make up and off I went. I made a few phone calls and grabbed a bottle of Evian out of the fridge, smiling as I left my house. I knew I looked butch in comparison to normal, but Samantha was in for a treat.

I stopped at all the places I had on the list and acquired the items I needed. I had a good time doing it and was quite pleased with myself when finished. I pulled up to her house again; this time I saw her forest green Rodeo in the drive. She was home, my heart leapt. I got my bags out of the trunk, the one I packed and the ones with my goodies in them and walked up the sidewalk to the porch, knocked lightly and went inside. It looked even more inviting in the daylight.

I rang her bell. This time it took awhile for her to answer. It was four forty-five, and I knew she was home, so I waited patiently. She finally came to the door. I was astounded. She had on a pair of faded jeans, and forest polo just like my navy one, with a white T-shirt underneath and boots. We looked like twins. I laughed as I looked at her. She was more beautiful than ever. I moved inside the door, dropped my bags and grabbed her immediately. I pushed her up against the door as she closed it and kissed her hard. I had actually missed her in the few hours I was gone. She had a different perfume on, Amarige; I was well aware of it, I wore it myself. I loved the scent. I immediately hit her neck with a barrage of kisses and moaned as I felt her tense up at my touch. She grabbed my head and held me close to her as I unbuttoned her oxford and kissed her lower and lower until I hit cleavage and was afraid I would rip her T-shirt if I pulled on it anymore. Back up her neck I went, kissing and sucking gently to her earlobe.

I whispered in her ear, "Hi Darling, I came back. Did you get my note?"

I could feel her nod as I nibbled on her ear. Her breathing had increased, her chest almost heaving as I pushed her up against the door harder and kissed her lips. My lips burned as hers pressed against mine, her tongue so much more intense today than last night. It's like we opened up a new avenue with each other. I was glad it had turned out as it did. She was still wrapped around my head and shoulders, holding me to her...kissing me and exploring my mouth with hers, her lips tracing mine, her tongue meeting mine and flicking my bottom lip softly.

"I should stop while I can," ran through my mind. Reluctantly, I pulled my lips from hers very slowly for effect. Touching her arms with my fingers, caressing them as I unwrapped them from my head and shoulders. She opened her eyes dreamily and looked at me. I saw such intense pleasure in them. I 'd never seen her like this before, even last night. She looked as if she were just coming out of a deep sleep. I took her hands in mine and brought them both to my lips. I kissed each and every fingertip and ran my tongue down her palm. I then kissed her softly once again. I took a deep breath and looked at her; she was smiling.

"I missed you, too..." she breathed in a husky voice.

I grinned bigger, my eyes lighting up. I reached down into my bag of goodies and pulled out a long white box. It had a green and white bow on it, and I handed it to her. She looked at me surprised.

"Open it, go ahead." I said.

She did and as she took the ribbon off, she opened the lid to find eleven white roses with one red rose in the center. She understood. I knew it when she looked at it, and took the red rose out and smelled it first. The white roses stood for purity in love. It made the one red rose more pure in its form.

After a long pause and a passionate glance, holding nothing back she said, "Come help me find a vase, please?"

Her reaction was so unlike the woman that ran the shelter, always calm, always professional; I liked the combination. We walked into the kitchen and she got in a cabinet for a vase.

She had impeccable taste, you could tell that by the items in her house. She ran water while I cut the stems and pulled the greens out and began arranging them. She brought the vase to me sliding her arms around my waist from behind as she placed the vase on the counter in front of me. I arranged the flowers for her awkwardly, with the red one in the middle; the stems cut just the right length so that all twelve roses were visible.

I had chosen the greens by hand for her and had picked evergreen and babies breath to enhance the white of the roses. It looked quite nice when I was through. She hugged me from behind, laying her head on my shoulder. Without disturbing her much, I turned in her arms.

"Is this comfortable for you? Me being here?" I said.

She never broke eye contact as she whispered, "Oh yeah. I love you being here. I've thought about you many a night as I stood here unable to sleep, wondering what your life was like outside the shelter. You're always so calm and cool there. I love the way you handle the women. Not many of the women there know that you are a lesbian, but I picked it up the first time I saw you." She said.

I must have changed my expression, because as she continued, her voice softened even more, "I saw you come in for the volunteer training almost a year and a half ago. You sat quietly, while we trained you. You watched me; I could feel it. You had an AIDS ribbon on your jacket, dressed so smartly, in your business suit. You're always either very casual or very dressed, no in between. I've seen you show up in shorts and a T-shirt, jeans and oxfords or in business suits. You always look as if you stepped out of a shower and show up fresh. Even though I knew that there were days you worked for over ten hours at your regular job and showed up for you volunteer work, you still looked fresh and crisp. I could tell what rooms you had been in at the shelter, your perfume, faintly lingered nearly driving me crazy. You wear Tommy Girl and I can't smell it anywhere without thinking about you. Do you know that I have watched you and thought about you for over a year? Do you know that?" Her mood became intense.

I didn't know that. I had been so caught up in not feeling in my life this last couple of years. "No, I didn't know." I said.

She looked disappointed for a moment and then broke into a genuine smile again. "I guess it's been worth it. I watched you trying to find something wrong; *one* thing that would make me quit thinking about you. I found nothing. So, after calling you again last night wanting to see you so bad, after not having seen you for a week, and worrying about you after we talked the other night, I called you to come in. I was so upset that you weren't home. I sat here for hours thinking that you might be out with another woman, my heart breaking into tiny pieces as I made the manicotti. I cook when I stress..." She tossed her hair back. "So, I finally called your work number. Taking a huge risk. When you answered, my heart leapt. I didn't know what to say. Miss Savvy here, I was speechless. And then you said my name. I melted. I wanted to feed you. When you said you would come over, I had no idea what to do. I had no idea if you knew I was a lesbian. Since I moved here, no one has seen me with anyone, there have been a couple of questions, but I'm lucky, I don't look like a lesbian. My staff knows everything, only because I told them; I didn't want them to ever find out any other way, working along side me so closely. Last night I just kept thinking about you and whether or not you were with someone else. I almost made myself sick." She said.

As she finished, I was even more speechless than before. The care in which she placed her clients and staff, her demeanor, her intensity and the way she spoke of me. I could do nothing but hold her close to me.

I leaned into her ear as I held her and said, "I am going to make love to you tonight, if you'll let me."

She said nothing, just held me tighter. I took that as a good sign.

I began to smell something. Her house smelled good but this was different. "Do you smell something, Sam?"

In an instant she was out of my arms, grabbing potholders and opening the oven door. Smoke slid out of the oven and she pulled out two Cornish game hens on a tray. They had a little crusty outer shell with smoke rolling off them. I was laughing. She didn't think it was funny though. She just looked at me as though she could cry. She placed them on top of the stove and turned the oven off. Hands on her hips, she looked at me again as she stood in the middle of the kitchen, like a little girl who had just broken her favorite toy.

"Aw, Darlin, don't cry, it's okay." I said as I walked to her. I put my arms around her and kissed her head. "I made some special plans too, maybe we can revert to mine?" I tipped her chin up to my face and kissed her softly, reassuring her that it was okay.

She started in again, quickly this time, "I was making us dinner and then I had some movies, really no plans, just wanted to be with you." She pouted and continued," I had so much to do today that I really didn't get time to plan, so I threw these game hens in and figured I could create from there, but you were back so fast and here I am, barely dressed. I have burnt dinner. *ALL BECAUSE OF YOU...*" She whined shamelessly, and then she laughed. We both laughed. She was like a child. It was so wonderful to see her like this, so real.

Chapter Four

"Let me take care of this evening, is that okay? Do you trust me?" I asked her in a soft voice.

"Yes, I trust you. What did you have in mind?" Her voice crawled to me, sultry and seductive.

I took her hand and led her to her bedroom, her eyes lit up when we turned into her room; I hated to burst her bubble, but said, "Not what you think, Darling. I need you to pack a bag. Can you afford all day tomorrow off? The whole day?"

She looked at me with admiration, "That would be fine. I don't have anything planned, actually I stopped by work and canceled what I had originally scheduled and took the entire day off. The girls were flabbergasted; wanted to know what was up. I played coy and wouldn't tell, but they kept telling me I looked exceptionally well today and wanted to know who *SHE* was." We laughed.

I said, "I canceled plans I had tonight and had intended to rest all day tomorrow and work on those numbers again, but I have made a big decision too. I am leaving the company. So, Monday I must begin looking for a job."

She hugged me again, this time like the worker that spoke to me the other night. I knew she had heard how much I loved my job and what this meant to me. But everything was going to be okay. I knew that. I didn't know how, but I knew it would be okay. I leaned down and hugged her.

"Pack a bag. We're going to take a mini-vacation, slash rendezvous." I said.

"What should I bring?" she asked, "I have no idea where we're going." She was milking me for information.

I didn't want to tell her or it would ruin the surprise. So I said, "Why don't you just let me help you pack? Would that be okay?"

"Okay, but, only if you kiss me first." She had that evil glint in her eyes. She moved slowly toward me.

I ran from the room; I ran stealth into the hallway and hid around the corner hoping she would come find me.

I heard her coming after me.

I screamed as she hit the door and scared the begeesis out of her, watching her throw her femmie little arms up in the air and scream back.

I grabbed her and kissed her again, grinding my hips into hers wanting to feel that closeness I experienced the night before. She moved in rhythm with me, moaning now, not screaming.

"Oh, wait, the bags...we have to pack a bag." I said, out of breath and completely out of control.

"Oh, yeah. The bag." She said and walked back into the bedroom, my hand in hers in tow we moved slowly and I took the chance to watch how her buttocks moved when she walked.

"Hey, quit looking at my butt!!!" She said and turned around. "No fair, Abby." She held her hands between her backside and my gaze. "Quit watching me..." She laughed.

She walked to the closet doors and threw them wide open. We walked in and after thumbing through some of her things; I saw the perfect outfit, a mauve and tan pinstriped pantsuit. It had the look for the restaurant I had chosen and made reservations at, so I pulled it out.

"How about this one, sweetie?" I tossed it to her playfully. Then I saw a great pair of flannel pajamas. I grabbed them; I didn't think she would need them, but had to be a lady about it.

"Here, you won't need these, but you might pack them anyway." I grinned.

She tossed them on the bed.

With a coy grin, I said, "You pick the rest, I just want to watch." I moved to the bed and sat back watching.

She grabbed a pair of jeans, two shirts and a belt. While she was grabbing

shoes and accessories, I told her I had some things to do real quick and left the room. I went back to the living room where I had more goodies waiting. In my bag, I pulled out a package that was wrapped, a small present for her; a bag of fruit; a new small cooler for the fruit; a bottle of Merlot, two wine glasses that were also wrapped in a gift box; and two tickets to the WNBA basketball game that night. I went to the kitchen and put ice in the cooler and chilled the fruit: grapes, oranges, apples, kiwi, and a pomegranate. I went back into the living room and put the wine and presents in my overnight bag and made sure my CD's were tucked in safely.

I had one more package left. It had a new portable CD player, candles and massage oil. I felt as if I were ready. I had everything tucked away when she entered the room. She had changed into a different pair of jeans and a pair of white sneakers. She still had on the matching Polo to mine. I was tickled with that.

"Looks like we're ready to roll…just one more thing." I said and walked to her and took her bag from her, carefully placing it on the floor.

I took her in my arms and began to dance.

She followed divinely, flowing across the floor when I led her away from me to spin her under my arm and then back. I kissed her.

"You are nothing like what I imagined and let me tell you, I imagined quite frequently." She said.

I pouted immediately and stopped dancing.

"Don't get me wrong. You are a thousand times better than I even imagined and my fantasies were pretty good." She smiled.

We got in the car and hit the streets. We drove hand-in-hand across town, listening to music and chatting lightly. She told me about growing up in North Carolina and I told her about Kansas. We talked about our families, our friends, what we loved and what we didn't about where we grew up.

"Oh, Shit!!! I missed the turn, I was so into our conversation." I turned the car back around and found the turn. About a mile later, we were at our destination both laughing and commenting on how silly we were being.

We pulled up to a rustic cabin. I said, "Friends of mine own this and rent it out on the weekends."

As we pulled up, you could see the cabin itself. The lake was the best part. Since it was mid-September, it was still warm enough out that you could be out back and not freeze. I had a couple of blankets in my trunk that were there all the time and my fishing equipment in case of an emergency fishing excursion.

I turned to her as she stood beside me while I dug in the trunk. "Do you like to fish? I love to fish." I had no idea what Sam liked, so I hadn't really thought about the lake part of the property until just now.

"I haven't ever really done it before. I watched people a couple of times, but I wouldn't mind you teaching me?" She said.

I grabbed the fishing equipment, the cooler I had packed and her hand after giving her the blankets and pulled her behind me like a kid not able to get to the lake fast enough.

As we broke around the cabin, half dragging our things, we saw the lake before us, I heard her whisper, "This is heaven; I have died and gone to heaven."

I just nodded in agreement.

We trekked down to the waterline and found a clear space to lay the blankets and got everything out. I pulled my rod out and put some stink-bait on the hook and tossed it in. Then I waved my hand in front of her face, knowing the bait was rank.

"Gawwwwwd, you stink now." She said wrinkling up her nose.

I laughed as I washed my hand off in the water, kneeling down about three feet in front of her.

The next thing I knew, I was face down in the water; she had pushed me from behind. I screamed like a sissy as I fell forward, nothing to catch myself.

"What the..." I said as I fell into the water with a splash.

I came out of the water spewing, gasping, having had my mouth open like an idiot when I went under. My hands were all muddy and I was sopping wet. I heard music playing as I came up.

As the water fell from my head and I got turned around, I could see her taking off her oxford and tossing it on the ground and kicking off her boots. She had gotten the CD player and had turned on music and was shedding clothes as she walked forward and let herself glide into the water and my arms simultaneously. Her lips hit mine with fervor unlike anything I had ever known.

I let us fall into the water to get her wet as we kissed.

"It's so cold." She said as she came up shivering.

"No, you have to be kidding." I chided. I was freezing.

She climbed deeper into my arms trying to warm up, but missed by a mile. It was too cold.

"I just saw you leaning there over the water, trying to wash your hands; and I couldn't resist. I just thought it would be fun to frolic in the water with you. I didn't think it would be this cold." She whined, her lips turning purple already.

I wrapped my arms around her, swishing my hands to get the mud off them in the water and held her tight. We kissed until it was literally too cold to stay in the water any longer.

"We have to get out of these cold clothes or we're going to catch pneumonia." I said.

We moved to shore and when we emerged from the water, a sensation shot through my whole body. She had taken off the oxford and had on only a white t-shirt and apparently she was *very* cold. I stopped her from walking at the waterline and my mouth hit her hard nipple immediately and I began sucking through the fabric. It was enough to bring her to her knees. We scurried to the blanket; my mouth never left her breast.

For about ten minutes, we were content but then reality hit. It was getting dark and colder by the minute.

"Let's go inside." She said in that husky voice again.

We grabbed all the things and headed for the cabin. On the front porch I looked under the third rock on the right, where Desiree said I could find the key, and sure enough, there it was. I opened the door, expecting to see dirt and grime and old rustic furniture; I was flabbergasted at the sight before me. Sam was right behind me and gasped out loud at the sight.

"Oh My God! This is beautiful." She whispered, grabbing me around the waist again, preventing me from moving while we soaked it all in dripping water on the floor.

It was very modern. The carpeting was white and plush with black fluffy furniture. It looked like you would sink into the couch, if you sat on it. There were two black, high-back chairs made of cherry wood and various tables spread throughout the house that were black lacquered enamel. We found brass lamps spread throughout; I went and turned on the one in the middle of the room, hurrying so that I didn't drip on the carpet as she headed the other way. It lit everything up. It was one open room. The only other things seen were a small kitchenette area and a door to what must be the restroom.

"Please, God, let it be indoor plumbing." I mumbled aloud.

Samantha ran right to the door I was looking at and must have been thinking the same thing as I did, she said, "I hope this is a restroom."

As she opened the door, we were both pleasantly surprised. It had a standup shower, no tub, but indoor plumbing. She came back to me, as I laid the bags beside the bed and took my hand.

She said, "Thank you, Abigail. This is so cool."

She reached her arms around me again and we kissed. There was nothing to stop this kiss; we had nowhere to be and nothing to do for twenty-four hours or more. It was a slow kiss, lots of exploration; she was still new to me. My lips sought hers as our tongues danced in delight. I pulled my lips from hers so that I could see her face. She moved her hands to my shirt and began unbuttoning; I still had on my oxford. In a brief moment we were pulling our shirts off; I pulled her T-shirt off and then she pulled off mine. She was so tanned. I could see tan lines under her bra. I still couldn't believe how beautiful she was.

Her hands flew to my sides, finally finding bare skin. She caressed my sides as she kissed my neck. My head tilted back, her kisses arousing my very being to her command. Her hands were exquisite. She touched me lightly as she sucked on my skin just below my collarbone. I had plans and this wasn't one of them. I had known that I wanted to make love with Samantha that night, but not yet.

"I have plans..." I said as I moaned when she moved her kisses to my breast. Over my bra she took my nipple in her lips and toyed with me. I nearly came right then. Her hand moved to my other breast and caressed as she played with my nipple, thoroughly enjoying herself, or so it sounded. She was moaning softly into her kisses. She was skilled and teased me to a point of near explosion. I placed my hands in her hair and pulled her off my breast gently. I looked at her with passion and desire. She moved her lips back to mine and kissed me again. This time it was hard, forcing my lips apart and flicking her tongue against mine. I was melting quickly. She demanded my response and she got it.

My hands ripped at her bra, the front clasp breaking and freeing her breasts, which I immediately cupped in my hands as I rolled her nipples in my fingers until she moaned and pressed her body against mine. I kissed her with as much passion as I had for her, extreme intensity; I needed her.

Her hands went as quickly to my jeans as mine went to hers, and we ripped at them until her zipper was down and my buttons were bare. We tore at them until they were lying in piles on the floor and I pushed us towards the bed, our lips never parting. Her tongue driving me crazy with it's wicked attempts to toy with mine. Just as I would find her tongue, she would pull it back asking for mine's reply. I licked her lips and sucked on her bottom lip as we fell onto the bed, me on top. I liked the position I was in.

The fall broke our kiss and we were both breathing hard. She was scooting backwards beneath me to the top of the bed...and I was chasing her. Her legs were strong and lean and I reached to touch them. My hand glided up her inner thigh to about four inches below her hip. She watched my hand, expecting more and not getting it. My hand moved slowly over her hip to her stomach, teasing, where I traced her ribcage and ran it down to her belly button; I made little circles while I watched her reaction.

"I like watching you react." I whispered.

I deliberately ran my fingernails up her stomach, between her breasts, up her neck to her lips. I placed my finger on her lips, where she took it into her mouth. It was the most sensual feeling, feeling the inside of her mouth. It made me wonder how wet she was and I was going to find out soon.

She yanked down the covers of the bed and climbed inside; I followed her. We were clad in only panties. The only light that was on was the lamp on the other side of the room; it was measurably dark where we were now. We hadn't said hardly anything since we arrived. I became very insecure for a moment. I didn't know if she was tired or if she had gotten any sleep or what time she had gotten up. I was so selfish sometimes, only thinking about me.

"What's wrong?" she said. The look on her face was blunt, she was hurt, and she thought something was wrong.

"I'm fine, Honey. I was just wondering if this was okay with you, if you were tired or had gotten..." my words were stopped by her lips, she grabbed me and pulled me to her. She rolled on top of me and I had no control left. She made love to me right then, until I screamed in ecstasy.

She made love to me over and over. She was just the right amount teasing, just the right amount forceful and even more importantly, ever so gentle and tender with me. When she was done, I made love to her. I took my time, making love to her until she could take it no longer. It was so sweet and tender, as if we had waited a lifetime to explore the inner emotional reality of each other.

When I finished, I crept slowly up her body with kisses to find tears running down her cheeks. I held her for a long time as she cried and I cried with her. We rocked gently after we made love, in each other's arms, side-by-side, skin-to-skin. Arms and legs intertwined. It felt like home. The emotional intensity so charged it brought us to tears.

Chapter Five

As her sobbing subsided, I kissed her head; kissed her eyes; I kissed her nose; I kissed her cheeks and then I kissed her lips softly. She opened her eyes and looked at me, differently than I had ever been looked at before. It was naked and raw, as if her soul were open to me. She was pure; I could see it in her eyes. She had pain from her past but she was okay; she was open to me and I saw it, somehow I knew these things.

She kissed my nose and spoke. "I have never been so pleased. No one has ever done that to me before. No one."

I didn't know what to say, once again, so I didn't say anything, I just smiled at her softly. We fell asleep like that.

I awoke a couple of hours later; still in Samantha's arms; she was still sleeping. I looked at my watch and it was almost eight o'clock. I was starving. I slid out from under Sam's arms and out of the bed, grabbing the sheet that was now on the floor to wrap up in. Sam stirred briefly and I covered her with the comforter that was also on the floor. She smiled in her sleep, but didn't awake. I went to the bags and got the cooler and went back to the bed. I wanted an Evian so badly. I hadn't brought any; so instead, I grabbed a piece of ice and sucked on it. I opened the CD player and put in one of my CD's as I sat on the end of the bed by her feet. Quietly enjoying the solace of the moment alone, I played my CD; it played softly as I sat there, not really thinking.

I got the gift out of the bag. I'd seen this object about three months ago in the window of the jewelers and had wanted to buy it for myself. But, it wasn't something I would wear. It was beautiful, but not for me. I ran my finger over the paper, silver foil, and the ribbon, purple satin. My senses were so alive from making love. I felt the paper on my finger and smiled as I thought about Samantha opening it. She stirred and mumbled something. I glanced at her just as she opened her eyes and climbed up beside her with the gift in my hand. Again, I kissed her lips softly.

"I love you, Abigail," she whispered.

I wasn't even shocked by her words; they felt natural. I lay on my stomach across the bed and handed her the present.

"Here sweetheart, I got you something this afternoon. Especially for you." I said.

She moved a bit to get comfy as she took the package and I lay beside her and watched her start to open the gift.

She stopped opening and looked up and me and said, "Can you go get my purse for me, Sweetness?"

I did, in an instant. I bounced over to where she had laid it, retrieved it and bounced back to the bed. I jumped on the bed playfully and got under the comforter with her. We snuggled up as she got into her purse and pulled out a similar package. She had gotten me something too? Her present was wrapped in gold foil and had a red bow, very tiny.

The package was about four inches long and about and inch tall. I looked at her intensely. This wasn't something I expected.

She handed me the gift and said, "You have to wait until I open mine; I want to watch you open this." She opened the package slowly.

I was going nuts.... "Hurry." I joked.

I wanted to see her face when she opened the sapphire and diamond necklace. It was made to lay flat and had chips all the way around in a six-inch diameter. One row of diamonds nestled between two rows of sapphires, one on each side. It was shaped in a curved "V" and would lie perfectly on her neck. When she opened the package and viewed its contents, I saw her eyes mist. One tear slid down her face. I reached up and caught it with my finger and kissed it. She was so sensitive.

"Open yours, please?" She asked.

I did. I tore into my paper, but opened the box really slowly. I was sort of scared. Inside my package, lay a bracelet almost identical to the necklace I had given her, sapphires and diamonds. I was dumb-founded. How had we done that?

"Now do you see why the tears?" she questioned. "I feel as though we are soul. From the first time I met you, I could tell how withdrawn from hurt you were. I thought I would never get in and yet, look at this...similar presents."

I nodded in affirmation as she took the bracelet out of the box for me and put it on my wrist. I then placed her necklace around her neck. Kissing it into place. She held my hand afterward and looked at me.

"What now, Abby?" She said.

I hadn't really thought much about it. Our reservations for dinner were at seven. I was beginning to become uncomfortable with the fact that she told me she loved me, even though it was something that felt natural. It had always meant disaster before in my life. I decided to just ignore it and go with the motions of the evening.

"Looks like we missed dinner. I made reservations for seven o'clock." I laughed, "And, I had WNBA tickets, my best friend is in town playing; we could get a shower real quick and see if the game is still on and catch the end of it. I wanted you to meet Erica."

She said, "I would like that, maybe we could grab something to eat. I am famished and I don't care what it is. I haven't eaten since before you got to my house last night, with the exception of the strawberries and cherries."

We got up and showered together, washing each other's bodies, careful not to arouse anything or we would never make it out of the room and we were both starving. Something about getting older and *NEEDING* to eat, as opposed to when you are younger and can make love for days without having to worry about it.

"We're just too old for all this." She laughed and sprayed

me with the showerhead while she did it. "You make me feel playful and young at heart."

"You make *me* crazy. Why didn't you say something to me before last night?" I asked.

"I don't know?" She had a very serious look on her face. "Perhaps I was just afraid? Last night I sort of said, 'Geranimo.'" She crinkled her nose.

She spoke again as we both dressed from our bags, "Nothing I ever want turns out right. I wanted to be an attorney in North Carolina. I had a bit of bad luck and well; I got the job with the Women's Crisis Center there and stayed. It met my needs. I always had thoughts that I would return to law school. When I moved here, I had the education and experience to work for the shelter and so I did. I needed a job and I liked what I did; it would do until I could return to school and take the bar." Her southern drawl was deep.

She continued, "Those plans have sort of gone by the wayside, because we are so busy at the shelter and I can't do both. I can't leave the shelter and I can't live and go to school without a job." She shrugged her shoulders into her shirt. "I do, however, plan to do it by the time I am forty." She laughed softly.

I realized I didn't even know how old she was.

"How old are you?" I asked.

"How old do I look?" She said.

I wasn't playing that game. You could really lose on that one. I kissed her again and begged her to tell me. She looked younger than I did and acted older.

"Well, my birthday is coming soon and I will be thirty-five." she joked.

"How soon is soon?" I asked.

"Around the corner." She blew me off.

"Are you going to make me beg?" I pleaded.

"I know you don't think I'm going to make it easy after you made me wait for this for over a year, now do ya?" She teased.

"C'mon, Sam, tell me, please?" I begged.

"Well, the truth be known, it's tomorrow, September seventeenth." She smiled.

I cracked up, "The secrets you would keep from me, if I let you. Are you serious?" She nodded.

Our fun and friendly chat stopped there though, because my pager went off.

Chapter Six

I had hooked my pager to my purse and it went off and broke the silence of the moment. I tore myself away from her to check it. I loved hearing her talk; her southern accent was becoming more prominent for some reason.

"That's odd, it's the shelter," I said. "Let me call them real quick, Darling." I moved to a phone in the other room and fell into the couch to make the call.

I placed the call to the center to find Miranda on the other end.

Miranda said, "Don't panic, Abby, I don't need anything not even you to come to work. We're planning a surprise party for Samantha tonight. I couldn't get a hold of you the last three days, so I resorted to paging you. Samantha would be disappointed if you didn't show up."

"Right, Miranda." I said, not wanting to spoil the surprise for Sam, laughing softly.

"What's wrong, Abby?" She asked.

I just laughed more. I moved away from earshot of Sam and asked Miranda "Does Samantha know about the party?"

She seemed caught off-guard, "No, she doesn't, we're going to emergency page her later. The party doesn't start until about ten, because some of the ladies have other jobs and everyone isn't required to be back to the shelter until then. We planned to page her after we got a hold of you and Sherry, the only two staff members that we hadn't contacted. Why?" she asked.

I blew off the question, "Is there going to be food or snacks there?" I asked.

"We have a cake." She laughed.

We were starving, my stomach growling on key, so I asked, "How about if you order pizza for everyone, my treat? And, don't page Samantha; I will take care of getting her there. She is with me right now." I had a Cheshire grin.

"Sam is with you?" She asked coyly.

"That's great. I will be there and we will take care of it all," I said as Samantha walked up with a curious look on her face. "OK, Miranda. I can do that. I'll stop by and get that and bring it by. Thanks for calling. See you soon." I hung up on Miranda so Sam wouldn't figure it all out.

"What was that all about?" Samantha said.

"Oh, it was nothing. One of the ladies at the shelter has a new baby and Miranda said that they couldn't find diapers small enough for the baby. She asked me if I could go out and get a bag of little bitty ones for them. I told her I'd be glad to do it."

I knew this lie was not going to fly, but hadn't time to make a good one. I hated lying; I wasn't any good at it. Every time I tried, I told on myself. But it was worth a try. I was lying to her already. Great!!!

"Okay, we can pick them up on the way to eat, sound good?" She asked.

I nodded in agreement to her statement and that was that. She acted like it was nothing, she believed me. She had to know the girls at the shelter could send anyone there or one of the women could go themselves. They had never called me before to do anything like that, but she seemed to have bought it.

We finished dressing, did our hair quickly and were out the door by a quarter to ten. I couldn't rush her, because then she would know something was up.

"I still want you to meet Erica. I played ball with her in college and now she plays for The Charlotte Sting." I said in the car.

I'd promised Erica I would go out with her; those were the plans I had canceled. Sam chatted on the way back into town, a twenty-minute drive to the Coliseum. She asked where I wanted to eat, so I lied again and told her I knew exactly where to go. She had her hand on my thigh as we drove and talked with her other hand as she told me stories of the center staff. It was as if she had them on her mind after the call. She had me laughing at all their nonsense. She told me about how they teased her so much to ask me out. Wouldn't they be shocked she said, when they found out? I laughed at that one. How was she going to react when we got there?

"Do you want me to go in with you to take the diapers?" she said.

"That'd be fine." I said.

"What if they know?" she asked.

I shrugged my shoulders. I had been in the closet for so long, it might feel good to come out for a while. But, there was one problem; maybe this might be a good time to address it.

"What if I want to take the job you offered me last week? How would you feel about that? I 'd be working along side you and what if this goes somewhere or worse yet, what if we attempt something and then it doesn't work out. You already left one place you loved because of a break up, what about this?"

She sat quietly for a moment thinking. I knew this was sort of out of the blue and that it really did have an impact upon her job. It even frightened me that I mentioned a more long-term situation. My throat tightened at the thought.

"I would love to work along side you on a day-to-day basis. I travel sometimes and I work with a number of different organizations, so I am not always present in the shelter," she paused, "I take my job seriously and you are the best person for this position."

I could hear her move into work mode. She eluded the self-confidence of her position, and she continued on, "I'm not afraid of working with you. I have no idea what might happen between us. I really don't know you. But, I know me. It is my place of career, not my place of employment. When Lauren left me, I was devastated, not because of my position, but because I knew she wanted to move on and I didn't. I couldn't handle having to see her with someone else. I really thought it would be forever. I don't know what you want to hear from this, but I still hold this offer to you, Abby, if you want the job, it's yours. You could help to make this center even better than it is and we could do it together. I would have strict boundaries at work, but other than that, we could take trips together and things of that nature. I believe this to be a 'cause', one I am willing to fight, with you by my side, and make it better for these women." She paused and ran her hand up my leg, "We could put you in a different office than the shelter, it might be hard to keep my mind on work with you there…"

I looked at her, as I pulled into the Coliseum parking lot and turned off my ignition. It was just after ten. I took her hand in mine and placed it to my heart. Symbolically, I wanted her to feel what she did to me.

"Samantha, I have been out of this game for so long, because it was just that, a game to many. You make my heart warm. My friends call me the 'Ice Princess,' because my heart hasn't been warmed in so long and you warm it. I want you to feel what you do to it. In the last twenty-four hours, you have made me see things I have missed terribly. I wasn't always like this. I was loving and caring and loyal. I had great integrity in my relationship. I do believe in forever, Samantha. I don't want a fling, I don't want a long term relationship, I want forever. Do you know what will make forever? Because I do." I stated.

I looked into her eyes as I said these things; I poured my heart into her hand as I told her how I felt. I had not thought these things in such a long time. I felt like she understood, when she leaned over and kissed me gently. She wiped the lipstick off my lip afterward with her finger and we climbed out of the car. There were no words necessary, once again she understood.

We jetted up the stairs, laughing like kids as we went, and entered the coliseum. The game had just finished and the crowd came barreling out the door. I grabbed Samantha's hand and headed towards the locker room. I had parked so that we were as close to the locker room as possible. As we approached the door with intent to enter, the guard looked at us like we were crazy.

I eyed him back and said, "Hi, I am Abigail Mitchell, if you go in and ask Erica or Coach White, they will tell you to let me in. You might look silly, but I know you don't know who I am, so I will understand if you have to go ask." I played as if I were very important and dared him to ask who I was.

I turned to Samantha and began talking about how we were going to work on publicizing the team next year and how we planned to show the proposal to Coach White on Tuesday back in Charlotte. I asked Sam if she had double-checked my flight arrangements; she was acknowledging that as the security guard tapped me on the shoulder, my back to him.

"You can go on in Miss Mitchell. I know who you are." And he smiled as he spoke.

"Thank you, Thomas. I really appreciate it." I spoke to him as we walked through the doors he so kindly opened.

With a big grin, Sam whispered, "How did you know his name, Abby?"

"He had a name tag on, silly." I laughed. I had read his name off his nameplate.

We walked into the locker room, the coach was in the office and the women were just coming in off the court. I found Erica quickly.

She screamed when she saw me. "What the Fuck?" She was freaking out in the locker room, attracting all kinds of attention.

The players quickly gathered around and wanted to know what was going on. Erica introduced me to all the players and I introduced Samantha. Sam's eyes were wide and her mouth hanging open half the time. I couldn't believe something this easy would impress her. I had gone to college with Erica and we had played softball on team together. She sat the bench mostly in softball, but she had made her efforts known on the basketball court. We kept in contact and always met up when she was nearby. I had canceled plans with her tonight to spend it with Samantha.

Erica, being Erica, right then made a big show, "So, Miss Samantha" she said in her best black southern drawl, "you are who I got dumped for? I cannot believe she dumped me. She has never, since I have known her, found anyone more important than myself. How long have you two been dating?"

With that, Samantha busted out in laughter and reached up and hugged Erica. Erica wasn't even fazed by it, she hugged Sam back and they laughed. I knew they would be fine because Sam was different; surprisingly enough, Erica rarely liked my lover's.

"Ummmm, well we have worked together for about a year and a half." I explained.

"Don't give me that. How long have you been lovers? Trying to evade my question, I don't think so." She said.

"A day." I laughed.

"Shit. A day. You gotta be kidding? She is adorable." She looked at Sam and Sam blushed profusely.

"I haven't been called adorable in a long time, thank you, Erica." Sam said.

Erica knew me well and knew what my plans would be and she wanted nothing to do with THAT.

"How long are you going to be here? I'm jumping in the shower and then some of us are going to go to the club. Don't s'pose you would wanna join us?" She asked.

"No, I think we have plans already. Can I take a rain check? I know I'll probably be having a little more time. I can meet you in a month or so and you will get my undivided attention. Deal?" I said.

"Deal. Sheesh, she dumped me for somebody beautiful at least." She winked at Sam.

I said goodbye for now and grabbed Samantha and out the door we went again.

In the car, Samantha asked if I had been okay canceling plans with Erica. I was quite fine with it. I wanted to spend time with her.

I noticed that now we were nearly an hour late to her party. I stopped along the way, told Samantha that I had to use the restroom and had to buy diapers, so into a convenience store I ran. I called the shelter real fast and told Miranda that we were on our way.

She point blank asked me, "Did she ask you out tonight?"

I didn't really know how to answer, so I said, "She will fill you in, I'm sure..." and laughed and hung up.

I grabbed some newborn diapers and for a brief moment wished I could use them. I'd always wanted a baby. I shook that thought from my head and pranced out the door.

I jumped back in the car and grabbed her hand. I leaned over to her and nuzzled real close to her ear...kissed her earlobe and nibbled until I heard her moan and then started to say, "Samantha, I think I could love you too" but, I didn't. I just kissed her.

I started the car again and whipped off towards the shelter. I put my arm around her and pulled her close. We made it to the shelter in record time.

Before we got out of the car, I asked, "Sam, how do you wanna handle this?" I gave her a chance to answer, but nothing. I then said, "I can just go inside and give them the diapers or we can both go?"

She was so close to me that I was tempted to just stop there and make love to her again in the car. Her perfume was invading my senses. She was running her hand up my thigh and her other hand was caressing mine. She was driving me wild. She was toying with me; I had a feeling she knew what she was doing to me, even if it were only a faint feeling.

"I want to go in with you, do you mind?" She said.

I replied, "Honey, I don't mind at all, but it's your work and..." I stopped in mid-sentence; I almost said that Miranda had already asked me about us. I was caught; she knew that I had stumbled on my words.

She said, "Abby, I already know they are planning this for my birthday, Shelby has the biggest mouth this side of the Mississippi River. I have known for a week."

I was confused as she laughed softly. She had left with me today; I could have driven her hours away and she would have missed the party tonight? I had no idea why she would have let me take her away for the weekend if she knew about the party?

She continued, "I knew it when you asked me if I had any plans tonight and I was more than willing to explain to them, than miss the opportunity with you. I wanted to be with you on my birthday. That's why I called you last night. I spent my birthday alone last year for the first time and I didn't ever want to do that again. I really didn't have many friends, none outside of work and I was home alone last year on a Friday night and I hated it. That's why I was so brave as to call you last night. I took a big chance. Even if we just watched movies I knew we could leave my house and go to the party. I didn't want to ruin the surprise, but when you said you had plans, I thought what the heck, I would enjoy you more anyway. They know I have no life and that's why they are throwing this party."

I squeezed her hand tighter and kissed her head. "Then I just spent $7 on diapers that no one needs." And we laughed again. Our laughter filled the car as we pulled up to the shelter.

It was eleven o'clock straight up. I couldn't believe we were late. Neither of us was accustomed to that. I took a deep breath and said, "I will follow your lead." I wasn't real outgoing around the staff anyway. So, in we went.

The shelter was at an undisclosed location. It had to be for the safety of the inhabitants. The women and children who came to the shelter were often beaten or running from a father or boyfriend. It was sad. Most of the women had restraining orders issued on someone and their location was silent for their safety, their lives depended on it. The shelter was located in a nice neighborhood and resembled all the other homes for the most part. It had to be that way.

As we walked up the sidewalk to the door, Samantha turned and looked at me and said, "They're going to be like vultures, the staff. Just seeing you with me, they are going to know. They have been giving me shit for a year. Do you realize that? Are you sure you're ready for this? The one thing these women here are is open." She paused momentarily and then looked at me pleadingly, " I am chickening out."

She grabbed my hand. I knew she needed reassurance.

"It's okay Darling, I can deal with this. Blow them off. You elude such charisma. Put on that work face and you will be fine. Take them by storm. Tell them nothing, just wink and leave it at that and have a great time." I said.

She squeezed my hand and knocked at the door. There was no entering the shelter without a knock; no keys were issued, because they could be copied. So we knocked and waited. You could hear them all inside scurrying around and bumping into things. Kids were yelling surprise already and people were shushing them. We were laughing as Miranda opened the door wide and everyone yelled surprise as we walked in.

It was a virtual balloon haven. There were balloons everywhere. The kids ran up and gave Sam hugs and kisses and the women of the shelter shook her hand and some hugged her. She was having a hard time putting on her work face though, I could tell. I could see tears in her eyes. She turned and looked to find me, caught me watching her and winked.

I turned beat red. I never blushed. Miranda came up to me and asked for help in the kitchen.

Yikes!!! I did not want to be alone with the staff. They were gonna grill me; I knew it. .

As we entered, I saw seven pizza boxes and grabbed one really fast. I was starving. I opened it and looked for just cheese. The first one had all kinds of meat and green things and white things...ick! I moved to the next box, and found what I was looking for. I grabbed three pieces of cheese pizza, two on my plate and one for Sam. I got another box out and grabbed the first kind there was and put another piece on her plate.

I asked Miranda, "Do you need any help?"

"Yes. We have a special project for you." She laughed.

"Okay, let me give this to Samantha and I'll be right back." I said.

I went into the living room, where there was still a crowd

around Sam and handed her the plate of pizza through everyone. She nodded thanks and I went back to the kitchen.

Miranda grabbed me as I entered and pulled me into another room by my sleeve, almost making me drop my pizza. It was a teaching room that had tables and chairs for the kids. In the middle of the room was a huge cake. The kind people jumped out of. I was laughing so hard.

"Who is jumping out of this cake?" I asked.

Miranda laughed now. "You are," she said.

"Oh no I am not." I quit laughing immediately. "Are you serious? You want me to jump out of this cake? You have got to be kidding?" I was not jumping out of this cake.

Miranda looked at me solemnly..."Please Abby?" She pleaded. "You are the only one who can do this. We tried to get a hold of you all week long," she whined, "and you *have* to do this; you just *have* to."

I was not laughing. There was no way I was jumping out of that cake in front of them, even for her.

What a couple of days. I might have done this in college, when I used to drink, but not now. I was too embarrassed just thinking about it.

"How do you propose that I do this? Miranda, I am too shy to do this...you are crazy, Darling." I said.

I couldn't help but give Miranda a hard time. She was so easy anyway. She was as much a romantic as I was. I had talked to her a number of times and she was always moving from one boyfriend to another, they could never keep up with her.

She was pouting as she said, "We thought that maybe you could jump out of it, because Samantha said that all she wanted for her birthday was you the other day." She was looking at me under her lashes.

I laughed so hard I had to sit on the desk. "She said that?"

Miranda got a big grin on her face, "Yes she did."

Just then I saw Sam walk into the kitchen, so I ducked out of the room and grabbed her hand. No one was around so I pulled her into the staff restroom.

"We need to have a lil chat." I said as I closed the bathroom door.

"What's wrong, Baby?" She asked.

I was wickedly grinning at her and asked, "Did you say you wanted me for your birthday to the staff?

She blushed. For the first time, she blushed for me. I kissed her long and hard in the bathroom. Where did this woman come from? Had she really wanted me that badly? I hadn't even noticed her. I felt terrible. She was so pretty and so sweet and just the right amount of attitude and I hadn't even looked her way.

She kissed me then. She kissed the thoughts right out of my head. "I can't help it if I have known what I wanted, for over a year!" she said. She laughed. "You're going to get me in serious trouble with you in here. What if someone sees?" she teased me.

I replied to her, "Okay, they want me to jump out of a cake for you. What am I supposed to do? I can't do that. I am blushing just thinking about it." I just looked at her as I spoke.

"Tell them that I already had you for my birthday...that will shut them up." She said.

I agreed, it probably would, but they had this big ole cake. What to do? With another deep breath; I said, "Okay, I'll take care of it. You leave first and then I will come out in a bit. I'll figure something out." I whined.

She darted out the door with a swift kiss. I waited a couple of minutes before I left. As I walked out, I shut off the light and turned around to Miranda and Shelby standing there waiting for me, with their arms folded over themselves.

YIKES again!!!

"What?" I said. I was laughing again, because I didn't know if they had actually seen Sam leave or they were just waiting for me in hopes of me jumping out of that cake.

Miranda took charge, "Come back in here, Miss Mitchell."

I followed them back into the "cake" room. They were, by far, too serious looking. I glanced down the hall and everyone was giving Samantha gifts. I wanted to be in there with her. But, reluctantly followed the girls back into the lion's den.

Miranda wasted no time, "We want all the gory details and we want them now," she said as she moved toward me and a big grin came over her face. She gave me a big hug and patted me on the back. Shelby was right behind her.

"I don't understand," I said.

Miranda looked at me like I was crazy. "Please, don't be ignorant and don't play *us* for ignorant. We saw Samantha leave the bathroom and when she did she glared at us and told us to leave you alone." Miranda was laughing.

We had been busted.

Miranda made it clear, "I want details." Miranda was Sam's right hand at the shelter. No one knew their job better than Miranda.

To calm their curiosities, I said, "Samantha asked me to come over last night and I did, nothing more, nothing less. There are no details. I took her to a friend of mine's cabin tonight, because I didn't know about the party. I didn't even know it was her birthday until this evening. Honestly, that is the truth."

They weren't happy with my explanation. They just eyeballed me. I laughed and said, " Samantha said I didn't have to jump out of the cake…" and I left the room. I looked over my shoulder as I left and winked. They both smiled.

I went back into the living area where Samantha was opening her last gift from one of the kids. He was a ten-year-old boy, whose father had beaten him so badly, that he could not speak. Tommy and his mother had been in the shelter for almost the limit of time allowed, and everyone had gotten to know them fairly well. The husband had moved the wife and son here and then beaten them both to a pulp and left them for dead. Neither had died, but both were a mess when we got them from the hospital. The mother was fine now, but the little boy would not speak. He had been in for therapy, but had not come out of it yet. He had all the parts to speak and the doctors believed that he could, but wouldn't. His mother had blacked out and the little boy had probably tried to kill the father and gotten it next, that was the best speculation, but Tommy didn't speak to confirm, so no one really knew.

Tommy and I got along very well. He liked my computer. When I would volunteer, he would come and get me and tug at me until I opened my computer up and let him play. Tonight he was taken with Samantha. He had given her a special gift, something he'd made for her. His mother was telling Sam that Tommy had worked on it all day long.

Samantha unwrapped it with great care. I was watching intently as she looked up at me and patted the seat next to her for me to come sit. I looked behind me to make sure she was talking to me, as I leaned on the doorway, but there was no one else there. Miranda and Shelby had moved into the room and taken seats. So, I went and scooted into the cushion of the couch next to Samantha. I could feel the warmth of her thigh next to mine and smell her perfume again as I neared her.

She unwrapped his gift ever so slowly. It was very delicate you could tell and he had wrapped it with such care and admiration. I looked at Tommy and he was watching Samantha open the gift.

Sam leaned down to Tommy and asked him, "Tommy, did you make this especially for me?"

He nodded. When he looked up at her, he caught my glimpse as if for the first time and got up from the floor to come sit on my lap. I wished that I could do more for him and his mother. They were good, Christian people, always helping others at the shelter, doing more than their share.

Chapter Seven

Tommy put his arms around my neck and kissed my cheek. He had such a big smile on his face; he then turned around to watch Samantha again. She unwrapped a small clay sculpture of a duck. It looked almost real. He had defined the lines of the wings. And he had somehow chiseled in features of the face. It was no more than three inches tall and was very defined.

She held it up for everyone to see and said, "How special it is to have someone spend so much time and effort on a gift. It must be filled with love and care."

Tommy was grinning from ear to ear. He held my hands tightly and I squeezed him in a proud hug. Samantha leaned over and kissed him on the cheek. He hugged her neck hard. When she was released, he grabbed the necklace around her neck, the necklace I had bought for her, and he admired it. He was trying to ask her something, but she couldn't understand what he wanted.

I thought he wanted to know what the stones were. I told him in his ear, "Those are diamonds, the white ones and sapphires, the dark blue ones."

He wasn't pleased with that answer and touched it again, almost pulling on it in frustration. He looked at Samantha questioning her with his eyes. In turn, she looked at me. I decided that I might as well try; I'd been someone he was close to.

I asked him, "Tommy, if I get my computer out of my car, can you type what you want to ask her?"

He shook his head no and looked at me as if he were in

pain. I didn't understand now. Everyone was getting up for cake and ice cream now and the room was abuzz.

"Tommy," I said, "ask her the question; I think you can do it. Can you do that? Can you talk to Samantha? I'll help you, I promise."

He looked at me and gripped my hands tighter. He looked so afraid.

"It's okay Tommy, I'm right here with you. Look how big I am, I can protect you, I promise. Remember last weekend when I was here and I watched so you could fall asleep. I promised you that I would be here and I was. You can do this. I know you can. Do you want to try?"

Samantha looked at me like I didn't know what I was doing.

The doctor had told Tommy's mom to try and get him to talk, that when he was ready he thought that Tommy would just begin to talk again. He didn't think it was a medical problem, but rather very psychological. Tommy wouldn't go to bed at night until after his mom was asleep and he couldn't hold his head up anymore. I'd promised him last week that I would watch his mother sleep and make sure she was protected and he finally drifted off to sleep, only when I promised to sit in the room. It saddened me that a ten year old had to protect his mother this way, but it was our reality here at the shelter.

Tommy leaned over to Samantha; he gripped my hands so tight that it hurt. He was pretty strong for a ten-year-old. He closed his eyes and mumbled something inaudible. He had spoken though. I heard it.

I held his hands tightly back and whispered in his ear, "Come on baby, you can do it. You can trust Samantha, she loves you.... come on, Sweetie; try again. I'm here and you're safe."

He leaned closer to Samantha even, putting Sam's head between his and mine to where she was almost laying her head on my chest. She tilted her head so she could see me. He said it again; Tommy spoke again. This time he said something about who and necklace. It's all I could hear.

Samantha moved back away from me, so she could look at

Tommy. She looked him square in the eye with the most love I 'd seen.

"Do you want to know who got me the necklace, Tommy?" She said.

He grinned real big and shook his head yes over and over. I was crying at this point. He had spoken; he'd said something. My emotions were so out of whack with all that had happened in such a short time. I was so excited I wanted to run around the room screaming that he had spoken. Sam looked at me with the same look that she had for Tommy.

"Tommy, Abby got me the necklace. She gave it to me today." He shot a look to me. It was eerie.

"I love you Abby," he said. Not a lot of it came out, but I could read his lips clearly. His little arms went around my neck and he buried his face in my shoulder and he cried. He sobbed and sobbed. I didn't know what to do. I was crying hard with him. Samantha had tears streaming down her face. We all just sat there. Samantha took my hand in hers and we cried.

This little boy's dam had burst and he was just sobbing as I held him. Sam asked one of the other children to get Tommy's mother. She ran into the other room and Tommy's mom came flying to where we were sitting. Tommy was audibly sobbing now, his voice returning after months of not speaking. She dropped to her knees in front of me and began praying.

She thanked God for us all and thanked God for all she had been given. She prayed and prayed thanks. Sam never took her hand out of mine. I stroked Tommy's head as I held him. I looked at his mother as if asking her did she want to trade places and take him. He was still sobbing. She motioned no with her head and stroked his hair with me. She talked to him softly as she told him how much she loved him. He was quieting now some. But he was still audible. I just held him. He became limp from the crying, without energy at that point.

Samantha just kept watching me as I held him and comforted him, her hand in mine. She was not ashamed at all. She leaned forward and kissed Tommy's head and kissed my head and got up. She went to Shelby and gave quick instructions and helped all the other children into the other room.

Everyone had begun to gather as they heard Tommy sobbing so loudly. He was quieting down now and Samantha had it all under control in a matter of seconds. I saw Shelby go into the crisis phone room and make a call.

I looked at Sam. She mouthed that Shelby was calling the shelter physician to have him come check out Tommy, just in case. I nodded okay. I tried to move Tommy a little bit, but he wouldn't let go of my neck. Samantha saw me try and move him and came to the rescue.

"Honey," she said, "Tommy...Babe, can you help me for a minute? I'm going to go put my duck in my office and I need a really special place to put it. I need some help finding that special place. Can you come help me, Sweetie?" she cooed.

Tommy heard her, because, through his hiccupping, he nodded yes. He loosened his grip a bit and that helped. My shirt was sopping wet with tears and nose leakage. That poor baby had sobbed for almost a half hour. He looked for his mother when he brought his head off my shoulder. He saw her and grabbed for her, the tears began to stream down his face and he sobbed once again.

"I'm sorry Mama. I'm sorry. I tried to kill him. I did, I tried." He buried his face back in my shoulder as I stood up.

"What?" She said. "Tommy..." She burst into a heart-wrenching sob. "Tommy...I am so sorry, Baby." She touched his face, pawing softly in appreciation and pain for what he went through. You could see that she blamed herself for his pain.

I held Tommy with one hand and her with the other as she held onto him as well. I looked for Sammie. She was standing about three feet away from us. She had gotten everyone out of the way and was still having a birthday party in the other room.

I knew what would break him out of this. I reached in my pocket, sliding Tommy up on my hip so I could hold him better and retrieved my keys. I handed them to Sam.

"Please go to my car and get into my trunk. There is a small key on here that is to my safe, and my computer is there, it looks like a spare tire compartment, will you get my computer case, Love?"

She was out the door before I finished the sentence. Tommy, hearing the word computer, pulled his head up again. He touched my hair.

"You love me, right Abby?" he asked me.

"Yes Tommy, I love you more than any other little boy in the world: I sure do. I even let you play with my computer, because you are the smartest and bravest boy I know. Aren't you?" I coddled him as I spoke to him.

His mother at my side, patting my back as if to say thanks you. He shook his head and moved his legs to drop to the ground. He took my hand and headed to the front door. His fears still prevalent, he wouldn't go very close, but we stood there, waiting for Sam to get back with my computer case. He hadn't left the shelter, the fear of his father returning reacting in an agoraphobic manner. As she walked in the door, his eyes lit up and a smile broke out on his face.

"Thanks, Sammmmanfa."

We all laughed.

I dropped to my knees and hugged him again. Sam took us through the crisis phone room and into her office. I had only been in her office three times before, all when she absent. It was nothing like her house, much more official looking, staunch. I opened the computer case and pulled out my laptop and fired it up for Tommy. He knew what to do and I let him go. Samantha walked up behind me and hugged me. She had no shame and I knew it was because of Tommy.

She whispered in my ear, apparently a little too loud, "I love you, Abby." and Tommy was right behind her, "I love you, too, Abby." He half yelled.

The doctor came in and watched Tommy play. He asked him some questions and seemed to be okay with where Tommy was. He asked that Tommy get another appointment on Monday to be sure, but said that he thought that everything would be fine. He still wanted Tommy in some kind of therapy, but that he seemed physically okay.

One of the staff members had taken Tommy's mother into a room and talked and made sure that everything was okay with her and filled out a report. She brought the report in for Samantha and I to sign and we signed off. It had been a long night. It was well past two o'clock at this point. Everyone had gone to bed. The party had been a huge success, as I understood it.

The staff had put everyone to bed and was in the kitchen drinking punch, soda and coffee and eating pizza. We went into the kitchen and everyone applauded lightly.

"How could I help but feel impressed with such a great staff?" Samantha said. We all exchanged hugs and tears again.

Everyone told Sam happy birthday and told us to go home. We hadn't even thought about that. We had to drive back to the country. I was exhausted and I knew Sammie had to be as well. We got our things and headed out the door, my computer in tow, for Tommy had fallen asleep. We had tucked him in and kissed him goodnight. I think his gift was definitely Samantha's best present.

Chapter Eight

As we drove away, I headed straight for Samantha's house. I was too tired to drive to the country and when I turned off on her street, she said, "Good idea honey. I am too tired to ride out to 'the farm'."

We laughed again. This time it was a tired laugh and she snuggled into my arm again as we drove. I was really tired. Making love had drained me physically and just the whole thing with Sammie had been a little emotional. Then with Tommy, that was draining. It was an emotional roller coaster.

We pulled into her drive; we both got our purses and got out. We walked onto the porch and into her house. She walked straight to the couch and fell on it...dropping her purse on the floor. I stood there watching her. She kicked one shoe off at a time and let them fall. She acted like she had a remote and pointed it at the fireplace as if it would magically pop on. I was laughing.

She said, "This is what I do when I get home from work. I pretend I have a handy-dandy remote and click it at all the things I want done when I am too tired to do them. You probably think I am nuts." She rolled to look at me when she said that.

I was untouched by it. I fell onto the couch beside her as she scooted to let me on.

"Get this. I walk into my house and start dropping pieces of clothing, one by one, on the floor. I don't even make it to the kitchen to feed my cat, just keep walking and drop into bed. I keep a pair of boxers and T-shirt on my nightstand so that I don't have to get into my drawers. I just fall into my bed and drop off to sleep. Sometimes I don't get my boxers and Tee on until halfway through the night. I work too much," I sighed as I finished speaking.

We just lay there. She kept clicking the remote, "Look, I just turned on the stereo." She clicked it at the fireplace, "It's on really low, I don't want to get us too hot; I'm so tired. I need to cool you off a little or you will wear me out." She laughed and clicked again, "Let's read a little. Here comes a book off of the shelf. And, the quilt to cover us up...we need..." she aimed the remote at the kitchen, "how about some more pizza?"

I laughed, "definitely more pizza." I snuggled in a little closer.

She clicked it a couple of more times, "popcorn and movies and...chocolate Sundays."

"You sure can use that remote." I reached to caress her cheek. "I love your eyes.

They are so beautiful, such vivid pools. I like the way the colors blend together and how you have that circle of gold on the outside." I gazed at her intently.

"You're too kind, Abby."

"I never thought I would ever meet anyone again. I think I had just given up. I hope I can be what you want me to be?"

"I just want you to be you. Nothing more."

We laid arm-in-arm for about twenty minutes and then I got the energy back to climb up, quite slowly, to my feet and drag her, even slower, to her feet.

"Happy Birthday, Sammie." I kissed her fully.

She had no problem getting her energy back at that point. She kissed me hard and passionately. She slid her hand up my shirt after ripping the shirt tale out of my jeans. She caressed my breast and fondled my nipples as she kissed me, her tongue flicking mine. She was like lightning; I didn't know where her hands were going to be next. She was kissing my neck, making me moan with delight when all the sudden, she reached between my legs and pulled her hand against me. I gasped.

"Oh My God!!!" I kissed her as her hands began roaming

my body again. I pulled away from her, walked with her hand in mine to the kitchen and opened her fridge.

"I hope you have some water." She did. I grabbed one for me and one for her and handed it to her. We then walked to her bedroom, this time me leading the way, towing her behind. It was as if I lived there; I just walked in and plopped on her bed.

She was smiling wickedly. I couldn't believe I had any energy left. Last night was so late and she was up so early.

"You have to be tired." I said.

She fell along side me in the bed, "Oh, I am. But, not too tired for this..." As she spoke, she lifted my shirt and ran her finger over my stomach. She paid attention to every part of me.

"Do you know how wonderful you are?" She asked. "I mean...you were so good with him. I personally have been working with him since he's been at the shelter and could not make any progress. The therapist he sees just keeps saying, 'in due time; in due time.' I kept thinking, 'In due time my ass.' I tried everything I could think of, reassurance, trust, you name it, I tried it and kept doing it. You do it with a damned diamond necklace and a computer. If I had only known." She laughed lightly and grabbed my breast again. As she fondled me, she spoke again, "I want to be a mother" the sadness apparent in her eyes, "I used to beg Lauren to have a child or adopt a child. We finally opted not to and I realized one day why. She just didn't want to be with me." She trailed off.

I brought her hands to my lips and kissed it.

"Do you know how I got this job?"

I shook my head no.

"I attended Duke University and got my first degree in Women's Studies and returned to pick up my Master's in Political Science, to be an attorney. I had been living in a relationship my first two years of undergraduate work, an abusive relationship. During the week prior to finals of my sophomore year she beat me so badly that I was hospitalized. In order to finish finals, I stayed at the shelter there and learned a lot about what abuse was and how, even in lesbian relationships, abuse existed. My girlfriend stalked me for the next year and on-and-off I had to go back into the shelter, because the threats were so bad against me. I had restraining orders issued and court orders to keep her away from me, but she would just break them. I lived in fear until I met Lauren. After I met Lauren, the other woman must have decided that she wasn't going to get me back. She left me alone." She leaned into me more and snuggled close.

She spoke softly, "After that, I attended workshops and ended up doing my thesis on the politics of non-profit organizations and their organizing bodies. I worked as a volunteer and finally attained the director's position a few years later, after completing my Master's. I stayed with them until Lauren broke the relationship off. I still miss it sometimes, my shelter in North Carolina," She had a forlorn look. "I help build that program from the ground up. Here I have a chance to do things I couldn't do there and I know it is a great opportunity. I have a proven track record and have the board on my side. The allocation of money is something that I can go to them and expect them to grant my wishes. That is completely different than in North Carolina." She looked at me as if reading my mind. "I asked them for the money to hire you, because I know that you could make this center one of the best financially funded in the nation. And if you could do it here, you could do it on a national basis."

She looked me in the eye and said, "I didn't do it because I wanted to date you, or whatever you call it. I did it for the center. I like what I see in you in more than one way. When you came in last Saturday and you were so tired, I knew something was wrong. When you told me your story, I almost wondered if there was Divine Intervention there. They were forcing you out and I needed you."

She looked at me lovingly. How could she not flatter me?

She then said, "Do you believe me?"

For the first time, I sensed insecurity. "I have no reason not to believe you, Sammie. I think I would like being at the shelter full-time and for good reason. But, I don't wanna talk about it right now, if that's okay?"

She kissed my chest where she lay and nodded. I stroked her hair. I moved under her and suggested that she come up to the top of the bed with me. I began undressing her as she stood on her knees on the bed. Slowly I took her clothing off, piece by piece as I kissed her body. Each part of her, I made love to. I caressed her and kissed her, making sure that I paid attention to each and every part of her that became visible under the clothing. I kissed her shoulders, her arms, her forearms, and her hands as I removed her shirt. I kissed her stomach, her ribs, her sides, and her back moving around her as she knelt there for me. I kissed under her bra strap as I carefully unhooked it from behind as I knelt behind her, letting it drop to the bed from her shoulders, caressing her breasts as she leaned back against me. My hands ran down her stomach as I kissed her neck. She laid her head back on my shoulder, her hair falling freely on my body.

I undid her jeans carefully and slowly as I nibbled and bit on her earlobe. I whispered in her ear, "Happy Birthday, Baby."

I pushed her jeans down as I caressed her body, moving my hands over her hipbones, over her panties, and down her thighs as she moaned. She reached her arms up and put them around my head, holding me to her as I kissed and sucked on her neck and shoulders, her perfume faint but intriguing. I leaned back enough that she fell on me and as we untangled our legs, I reached up with my foot. I grabbed her jeans with it and pulled them the rest of the way off. With her lying on top of me, her back on my stomach, I made love to her again. This time so slowly as I talked in her ear, telling her what I was going to do next, making her anticipate it and then teasing her. She moved her hips against mine wildly in rhythm to a beat we created.

Her moans were driving me to a point of no return. She was so urgent in her need, my hands playing her like a musical instrument. It was passionate and unique being with her. We spent the next three hours making love, slowly and sweetly, our bodies coming together, sweating, grinding, and moving in sync; our skin burning into each other, listening to her every sound, feeling for her reaction from my hands, my lips, and my tongue.

Making sure that I was learning her body as I went along. And she mine. Again, we fell asleep in each other's arms, completely spent. This time I kissed her to sleep.

I awoke the next morning, to the sun again, coming in the window. This time Sammie was still in the bed, but when I opened my eyes, she was awake, watching me sleep. I was blushing right off. I leaned up and kissed her cheek, "Morning, Baby."

She grinned. I stretched underneath her, arching my back to remove the kinks the sleep had left. I opened my eyes again and she was still watching me, so I rolled up onto my elbow and put my face in my hand and watched her back, mimicking her.

"Just how dorky do I look when I sleep? Do I snore? Do I sleep with my eyes open or anything weird?" I was pretty self-conscious at this point.

She replied, "No, you're beautiful. You sleep so peacefully, so quietly. Your face becomes as soft as a baby's. I just watched you sleep this last half hour. I fell asleep before you did last night, in your arms. It felt wonderful. This has been a great birthday."

I just gazed into her eyes. I, for one brief moment, felt as if I was falling in love, but the picture that entered my mind of what someone could pretend to be pushed the feeling right back out. One step at a time, I told myself, one step at a time. Don't be fooled again ran through my head. I would use this for what it was worth, but I wasn't going to be the fool again this time. It didn't matter how I felt; I had a bad picker. I had picked losers in the past. It would be some time before I let that guard down again. Confusion struck, for everything I hadn't known the night before, I was learning that I had known. Even though I didn't know Sammie in the way I had come to know her the last two days, I had known her from work. She was really herself there I just hadn't seen it. Her softness with the clients in crisis, her strength in taking charge, her wisdom at knowing when to accept and when to change things. I *had* known her. Even being uncomfortable in my head, I was comfortable where I was.

"Am I what and who you thought I would be, Sammie?" I asked.

She leaned forward and kissed me on the forehead.

"Oh, my yes. You are all that and more, Abby. And, no one has ever called me Sammie. I like that. I have been most pleasantly surprised. I thought you would be gentle and tender, but you are so much more. You are so demanding, but never forceful, just like with Tommy last night, you prod me along, gently but with encouragement. It keeps playing through my mind, how you got him to take a risk, to say what he needed to say. You were so amazing. I fell in love with you again at that moment, the moment he took that step for you, and you held him like you did. I fell in love with you again. When you made love to me with the same graceful charm last night; that made me want to fall in love with you over and over and over, Abby. I want you to give me the chance to be a part of your life in that way."

She reached up and touched her necklace again. "I love my gift. Thank you so much, Abby."

I let her move into my arms as we lay there. We talked half of the day, with intermittent love making sessions. I could not get enough of her.

Finally, I broached the issue of food, "Honey, I have to eat. Do we have anything or should we order in?"

"Let's see what I can scrounge up." She said and slid out of bed. "Oh, Lord, it's after two."

"You are even more beautiful today," I said.

She stood in only her long sleeved button up oxford that she grabbed out of the closet.

"If I don't leave now, we won't eat again." I smiled wickedly. "I'm going to go freshen up, Darlin. Be right back." I left for the bathroom where I freshened up my hair and all the best I could.

I got back to the kitchen and noticed she had tucked her hair up in a hair-tie; it hung in a long ponytail, "You look twenty." I said.

She was busy toasting bagels, cutting cheeses, slicing fruit and preparing a virtual smorgasbord. There were crackers and summer sausage, olives and pickles. My mouth was watering.

"I can take over, if you want to freshen up too?"

She exited with a little bounce-step.

I finished the snack-tray and moved it into the living room. I found a remote and opened the cabinet to her television. I looked through her collection of movies and found Gone With The Wind and stuck it in the VCR. I loved that movie. When she came back, the movie was just starting.

She had brushed her hair a bit and it was back in the hair-tie. She sat down on the couch and then got up.

"I have a better idea," she said.

She disappeared and returned with blankets and pillows in her arms and threw them on the floor. We grabbed the big couch cushions from her other couch and tossed them on the floor and made quite a little pallet. We climbed in and I sat the tray on the table next to us. I fed her fruit and she fed me crackers and cheese.

"Everything is better with you, Sammie." I said.

We played the rest of the afternoon, mostly making love. The movie ended and rewound itself and popped off and she grabbed a remote and clicked on the CD player, turned it up really loud and well, it was even more exciting making love to her hearing the music and the sound of our lovemaking mixed together.

She fell asleep momentarily and I slid out to the phone. I called in dinner reservations for six o'clock at the Copa Demaio, a great Italian restaurant. I also called my friends that I had rented the cabin from, Desiree and Jenny, and asked them if they would be so kind as to go out to the cabin, they lived a mile from there, and grab our things and meet us for dinner. They agreed and accepted the dinner invitation. I told them it was Sammie's birthday and they asked what to bring. I gave them a hint after they gave me the third degree as to what she had already gotten. They were like that; they would not show up empty-handed. And, they were too kind and well known to be shown up.

I went back to where Samantha lay and slid my legs under her head as I sat Indian style. In her slumber, she cuddled up in my lap, resting her head and one arm on my legs. It was about three o'clock and I probably needed to wake her up so she had enough time get ready before dinner. Her auburn hair swept over my legs and I remembered just hours before when she purposely made her hair run over my legs from my toes to my hips. She kept commenting on how long my legs were and made them come alive as she teased me with her hair before making love to me again. She was so into her lovemaking. While she was concentrating on one thing, her hands would be caressing my body, each and every part of me. I felt things that I had never felt before. I had always done that, never stopping too long in one area, but moving around my lover's body so that they were always experiencing touch of a different kind. Samantha was wonderful, and never did the same thing. I used to tease my lover that I felt like a virgin, because every time felt like the first time for me. But, it really did with Samantha. I had one lover, we were together for quite some time and she was so inhibited. She rarely did anything different, same time, at night, only before going to bed, no lights on, no music...it was so monotonous. I hated it, but I loved her and didn't want to hurt her. I was glad for that relationship to be over.

My thoughts came back to the present, when Sam's hand ran up my thigh and under my shorts I had put on. Yeow! I jumped. She was so wicked sometimes. She looked so innocent just moments before and now this. She was toying with me. She wouldn't stop, and it felt so good, who was I to ask?

Ten minutes later, as Sam climbed to sitting and held me close to her, I remembered the dinner reservations. I knew we both needed to shower and that I had nothing to wear here. We might have to go home; or we could go shopping together, which didn't sound like a bad idea.

I broached the subject with Samantha, "Hon, I made reservations at Copa Demiao. Is that okay?"

Her eyes lit up. "How did you get reservations there, with this kind of notice? I had tried for three months to get reservations there and could never do it."

She sounded astonished. I hadn't thought it any big deal until she said that.

"Our company has a private table there and we eat there so much with clients that they know me pretty well. I've entertained many clients at the Copa. It's right up my alley. I'm vegetarian and it was nearly impossible to get food without meat. And, I'm a weird vegetarian at that; I hate the weird vegetables. I only liked corn, green beans, peas, potatoes broccoli, cauliflower and carrots. The Copa makes veggies just for, carrots and broccoli. Because of that, I go out of my way to have their pasta; they had the best." I said.

She slid around to where she was in my lap, but her back was to my front and my arms went around her, instinctively, to hold her close, her perfume still invading my senses, even though it was faint now.

She wrapped her arms in mine and asked, "Can we talk, Abby?"

I loved the sound of her voice and her southern accent. And, so far, I liked what she had to say. "Sure, Sam." I said.

She began the conversation right off with her point, "I have made a decision. I felt that I am entitled to this decision, being the corporate executive of my own world..." She didn't laugh.

I was laughing as she said this, even though she was serious.

She asked me, "If you take this job, would you be opposed to possibly having office space in a downtown office, rather than in the shelter? I feel as though you are not used to the shelter environment, but rather the office environment. Yesterday, while I was out, one of the places I went was to an office that my friend, Monica, has. She does corporate attainment for local and regional events on a national basis. I spoke to her about you, Darling." At that, she turned her face towards mine to see my reaction.

"So far I am impressed and think it sounds like a good idea. But, I have to think about it." I didn't want to talk about work. I kissed her forehead. "Would you write her name and phone number down and I will make an appointment with her this week and see what it brings?"

She smiled, her eyes lit up and she turned around. "I thought you would be mad at me. She got married the first of this year, and I haven't seen her much since then. I met her at a National Association of Female Executives conference in San Francisco last year, right after I got here and we ended up living in the same city. It was kind of cool." She said. "I just thought it would allow us some anonymity in our relationship."

I felt that familiar tinge of fear shoot through me. "Sammie, what do you want out of a relationship? I mean what do you play through your head with me? How does the dream look? You have one, don't you?"

She moved around, pulling away from my arms to turn and sit on her legs in front of me. She looked down at my hands, now lying in my lap and took them in hers. She brought my hands, one at a time to her lips, and kissed them softly, her eyes closed. Then she lifted her head and opened those greenish-blue eyes, with her long, dark lashes looked at me.

Her eyes bore into my soul. She said, "Abigail, I want to marry you some day. I want to have children, a home; I want to work to make the shelter a better place for the families that need it. I want to travel and speak with you at seminars on abuse on how they can market their program to reach the most closed off and abused individuals. I want to bring women and men to awareness that abuse doesn't have to happen, with you by my side. I want to raise babies. I love children and have always wanted to be a mother. Lauren said she didn't want to do that with me," her eyes misting, "I really want to be a mother. Abby, last night when you held that baby, when you prodded him to talk, something professionals couldn't do, I knew that I could raise children with you. I knew that you had what it took to be a parent. Not just to want children, but to be able to handle it too. I fall in love with each part of you. I can't say that this will work out," her look at me so intense at this point, "but I would like to give it a try."

She was silent after that and her eyes dropped to my hands again. I took a deep breath, something that brought her eyes imploringly to mine again.

"Sammie, I want that too, all those things. I want to grow old and sit out on this porch and drink lemonade as the grandkids play in the yard. It takes more than love Samantha, so much more than love. You barely know me. I barely know you. How do you know it isn't just that you want this to happen with 'someone', rather than me specifically?" I asked.

With that, my eyes dropped from hers. I couldn't look into them as she spoke the answer, because she might admit that it was just anyone, and not just I.

"Abigail, you're different. You've taken on many issues in your life and beaten them. I listened to you talk to Shelby one night after taking a call; I was leaning on the doorway outside the office and heard you talking about your father dying. I heard the love that you have inside you for others, and most importantly of all, your family. I've been watching you. I've been listening and watching, learning who you were for a year and a half. In that time, I have examined who I am. It was hard to define a 'me' again. I had been with Lauren so long. When I mention her name, you don't react. It's like you let me have my past and my present. You asked me what I wanted and I told you." She said.

With that, she tipped my chin to her and kissed me hard and soft at the same time.

"I can't explain that kiss, but there were no hands anywhere else on my body, and yet you lit my entire being up. A flame began burning inside me." I said, knowing that flame had flickered prior to that. I had fallen in love before and had done the same thing. I had been oblivious and then just fallen like a rock when they looked me in the eye. I had to look deep though and see if there was a soul in there to even reach for. I believed in karma and souls and forever. I believed in a world better than the one we're in and I believed that people were meant to be. Past lives and future existence all encompassed this life. I had met people before that I knew. I *KNEW* them; I didn't have to get to know them. She was one of those people. I could anticipate her actions in thirty-six hours. I went from being afraid of her to feeling safe with her. Tears slid down my face. I began sobbing for no reason. All the years of pain I had held in were released and I just sobbed as I fell into her arms.

She began sobbing too. She tried to speak, "Abby, sorry, I didn't mean to make you cry. I am sorry for being so pushy," she said as she choked her way through the words, "I didn't mean to offend you. I am sorry."

She kissed my head as she said these things apologetically. She had misunderstood. She thought I was crying because I didn't want those things.

"Sammie, Babe. Look at me." She crawled to my shoulder and held her head there hard. She wouldn't look at me.

"Look at me Sam, please." I was trying to move her head away from my shoulder. She wouldn't budge. We were both sobbing uncontrollably.

"Sammie, listen to me," I hiccupped through a sob. "You don't understand. You didn't let me speak. I am home Sam, I feel at home. For the first time in seventeen years, I feel at home." I was sobbing again, the words barely recognizable. The tears streaming down my face as she pulled her head away from my shoulder and looked at me, tears dripping from her lashes. She had a question in her eyes.

I whispered, "I am home. Do you understand? I haven't had a home since my father was killed when I was seventeen years old. I'm home, and it scares the shit out of me. I know what it feels like to lose home, to be abandoned."

We held on like this was our moment, nothing else in the world existed but us. We kissed for our pain, to relieve it; we kissed for the love that would develop between us in the years to come; we kissed for the long lost parts of ourselves that were sometimes missed; we kissed for the new relationship that was unfolding before our eyes; and we kissed for the passion that burned deep in the pit of our beings for finally finding each other. And, we held each other tight, because we knew the pain of the 'forever dream' being a fantasy.

Chapter Nine

We approached the restaurant hand-in-hand. Samantha had on a beautiful gray dress with a purple and mint print. It was very flattering to her figure, her tiny waist and her full breast; they were not large, but they were full against her tiny waist. She had on deep gray pumps and a light gray stocking. I had watched her dress, amazed at how quickly she did it; she accessorized in moments, something that took me days to do. She had gone into the bathroom, while I was dressing, and come out twenty minutes later looking as if she had walked off the cover of Elle. She was so classy; I loved that about her. She was the kind of woman you could take anywhere. She fit each part.

I prided myself on being able to throw my body in the dirt playing volleyball or softball and then showering and putting on a skirt and heels and doing just this, dining with friends. It was a good thing. She walked lightly; swinging her hand and mine was we walked from the car to the door of the restaurant. She stopped about five feet from the door and gasped out loud as she looked at the horizon. The sun was setting and it looked to be a blazing ball of red, yellow and pink as the horizon swallowed the ball of fire.

She squeezed my hand, "We are lucky together, you know?"

I was sort of surprised by that statement. Lucky? Oh, well, she wasn't bothered by it. I sure did like her. I found myself just floating along with her. It was like being on a cloud. My life had been so frustrating right up until I had lay in the bed with her Friday night and slept in her arms. All the trash washed away and it just felt good.

We walked into the restaurant, without holding hands, it would not be respected inside and we knew that.

"Gerard, how are you?" I said as we approached the host stand.

"Miss Mitchell, what a thrill to have you dining this evening. And, to what do we owe this pleasure?" He asked, a flaming fag.

"I think I made that clear when I spoke to you awhile ago. Is my table ready?" I was being coy. I loved Gerard.

"Well, of course it is. And, your dining companions are already here, a flavorful pair. I seated them myself. Are you going to introduce me?" He asked.

"Gerard, I would like to introduce you to Samantha." I said, pulling Sam gently forward with my hand on the curve of her back.

"Mademoiselle Samantha, we hear this is a special day for you, and your friends have something special planned for you." He was such a ham. He kissed her hand and said, "Happy Birthday."

He escorted us to our table, chatting lightly about the menu and how he felt Samantha would enjoy her birthday. He leaned to help pull out Samantha's chair and I waited for him to pull mine next.

He came next to me and as he pulled out my chair to seat me, he whispered, "Lord, Darlin, you have excellent taste."

I had known Gerard was gay when I first saw him, but he had never acknowledged that about me before. I looked at him as I sat down and he winked at me and touched my shoulder as he greeted us as his wonderful women and his most favorite table of the evening.

"Might I make it more special?" He asked. I had already told the restaurant what I wanted done, when I made reservations and I knew that he was aware of that.

He then walked back over to Samantha and took her hand in his, kissed it and bid her happy birthday once again and off he went.

I had really enjoyed making the dinner arrangements and

knew that they would be so much fun and so nice. I hoped Samantha would like them as much as I did, but I was such a kid at heart sometimes. I had not had time to get her a real birthday present, and the necklace had not been intended to be that, so I had requested that someone use my credit card and have a present delivered to the restaurant. I gave specific instructions as to what I wanted.

It had been a chore explaining to them what I wanted, but they knew me here, I tipped well. I had worked as a waitress before and knew how respected my clients were that were tippers. It made the work well worth the effort. So, the Copa took good care of me. I scooted my chair closer to Samantha's, so I could grab her hand under the table as I made introductions to Desiree and Jenny.

"Samantha, these are my dearest friends, Desiree…" as I pointed to Desiree. "Desiree was one of our state congresswomen. She ran for political office when we were in college and, this is her partner, Jenny. Jenny is an exquisite artist."

Desiree's family had money, prestige and power and she had moved into politics easily. When she came out to her family, however, she had been cut off. Her life had shattered under her nose. She had told me this story one night after she first met Jenny at one of the gay clubs here in town.

Samantha said, "I know who Miss Carlton is, we've worked together before on some lobbying efforts."

Des stood up and shook Samantha's hand, "Nice to see you again, Sam. It's always a pleasure to see you. I didn't realize that you and our lil Miss Mitchell were acquainted?"

She had that sly look as she glanced my way and I said, "Oh Des, down girl. I'll tell you all about it later, at least let her enjoy dinner."

We all laughed. Des was so inquisitive and I knew she would not stand for not knowing what was going on. She kicked me under the table after she sat back down and told me thanks a lot. We were still laughing.

Jenny and Samantha stood half out of their chairs and shook hands politely.

"Nice to meet you, Jenny," Samantha said and Jenny returned the greeting.

We made light conversation for about ten minutes, talking about the work situation, how the re-election was coming for Des and what Jenny was doing at the Gallery. Jenny ran one of the art galleries in town and was a prominent 'starving' lesbian artist. Her works were great and I had purchased two of her sculptures for my living room. She really was talented. She stayed mainly in oil, which was not my favorite, but I loved her sculpts.

Out of the blue, Des and her big mouth came up with, "So Abigail, my sweetest friend...we have been calling your house for two weeks, no answer, no return calls, nothing. And then you call Jenny, not me, because you know I can't keep my mouth shut and ask for the cabin for the weekend. I think we are entitled to a little history here." She had a grin on her face from ear to ear, knowing that I would be embarrassed.

But, I fooled her, "Well, Miss Carlton, I gathered that you didn't check your office machine, or with your secretary, because I returned all calls to the office, where she informed me that you were not available, even for the ever popular Miss Mitchell. Am I right?"

She laughed out loud at that one and I could hear Jenny and Sam laughing lightly, not really knowing how "in jest" we were.

"OK. You win; I didn't check messages the entire week. I've been working on the re-election and it's so boring taking all the calls from the money-hungry hounds that I just blew it all off."

She grabbed my hand and squeezed it, "We worry about you, Abby. You are such a little loner and we never know where you are. You are so unlike our other single lesbian," she drew out the word to make it more lezzzzzzzzzzzzzzzzbian, "friends, who are so ecstatic when we introduce them. You never let us have any fun. So, Abby, quit making us wait...how did this happen? Last weekend you were beside yourself and now this?"

Samantha took her cue and grabbed the conversation, "Well, Desiree, I'm afraid this is all my fault. You see, I've been trying to get Abigail's attention for over a year now and finally, Friday night when I called her for the umpteenth time to come work at the shelter when she wasn't needed, so that I may look at her and at least smell her perfume...She didn't know I existed...she wasn't home. I worried for hours, making manicotti and all kinds of things to bide my time, when finally I decided to take the bull by the horns. I called her at work, and do you know that she was there? It was one in the morning and she was still at work, on a Friday night!" as she said this, she moved her hand to intertwine her fingers in mine under the table. "I was glad she was there. I thought she might have been out with another woman...so, when she wasn't, I invited her to my house then and there, for an after midnight dinner. And, she came." Samantha said. The candle flames danced off her eyes as she spoke with such enthusiasm.

Des and Jenny were speechless. "Friday night? You two didn't get together until Friday night? The way you spoke on the phone yesterday, I thought..." I now kicked Des under the table.

"Ouch, Abby."

We all laughed.

After that, the conversation lightened and we ordered our dinner. We shared a bottle of Forest Glenn Merlot and picked off a plate of appetizers. It was fun. They were holding hands under the table too; I could see Jenny's arm reaching.

No one at the restaurant paid us any attention and it was nice. We ate so much that we all sat back when we were done and decided that dessert was definitely out. The food was luscious. I had suggested to Sam that she order the linguini with clam sauce. She had and had even made me taste it off her fork, something I had found so sensual. I liked her feeding me; it brought back such sweet memories of that first night. And I had ordered Fettuccine Alfredo.

"I love the food here. How is the lover's delight?" I asked.

"It's great. I can't pick between the three kinds of pasta

and four sauces, I feel like I'm at a buffet table." Des said. "We haven't really eaten here that often. The bread sticks melt in your mouth and the steamed veggies are the best."

After our waiter cleared our table, we began conversing about the shelter.

Des asked, "Is there still a need for lobbying at the shelter?"

Samantha explained, "There is always a need and if you want to, we can set up a meeting next week and go over some of the particulars?"

A violinist came to the table. He told Sammie Happy Birthday and played a sweet serenade for her. It was beautiful. She was again, holding my hand under the table. The strings sang for her. I did not recognize the song, but the violinist played with grace and skill. We all clapped in delight when he finished. He bowed for us and kissed Samantha on the cheek before he turned and walked away.

"How are things at the gallery, Jenny?" I asked. "Aren't you doing an elaborate show right now?"

Jenny replied, "The artist is Russian and has such intensity."

As Jenny spoke, in her quiet manner, I felt Samantha's hand leave mine and move to my thigh. I had not expected it. She moved her hand slowly us the inside of my thigh, slowly and deliberately. I had on a forest green tight skirt that was slit up the front center. It wasn't slit very far, maybe four inches, but somehow Samantha had her hand on my bare leg and was traveling upward. It must have been the way I was sitting, the skirt must have ridden up, because Sam's hand didn't stop until she touched me.

Oh, my God. I almost jumped out of my chair. Jenny was talking about the gallery, Des was asking questions about the artist and Samantha was making me wetter than was a good idea. In the middle of the restaurant, she was caressing me. I began to sweat. I wanted to moan so badly.

I closed my eyes for a moment, just in time to hear Des ask

me, "Abby do you and Samantha want to come to the gallery showing after we get through here?"

Jenny followed her with, "We are having a private viewing of Tabrai's newest works. We would love for you two to accompany us, if you want to."

I opened my eyes quickly; they were all looking at me. A bead of sweat dripped down between my breasts. It was really hot in here! Sam wasn't stopping, quite the contrary, she moved her hand hard against me, almost made me gasp. My panties were ruined and I seriously doubted whether I was going to make it either.

"I, uh," I looked at Sam pleading for help with my eyes from her, "I don't know. Sam, what do you think?"

She was smiling shyly, "That would be great. I think we would like that."

I was sweating, no perspiring as a lady should term it, but I was sweating at that point. She had been doing this for five minutes and I was losing my cool here.

"Okay, that would be great." I choked out the words. I reached under the table and grabbed Sam's hand. I didn't move it, just made her hold it still for a moment. I knew Des had caught on, by the way she was grinning at me.

"Hot in here, isn't it Abby?" Des loved this.

Samantha retreated with her hand at that point and I looked at her. She knew she had been busted and she grinned at Des. I got up from the table quickly, grabbed Samantha's hand. They laughed.

I was so embarrassed. She was going to pay for this. I smiled at Des and winked at Jenny. "We will be right back, can you excuse us?"

Sam was moving to her feet as I began to drag her with me, dropping her hand as she stood. The girls were laughing hard now.

They were not shy about it at all, "Take all the time you need, we have some things to plan anyway." They were still laughing as I walked away, knowing that Samantha was directly behind me.

The restroom at the Copa was way in the back. I had to walk, dripping on myself the whole way, across the entire restaurant. I was beat red with embarrassment. I couldn't tell what Samantha's expression was, but I could hear her giggling softly as we walked, her heels clicking in time behind mine. My favorite forest skirt and my mint green silk blouse looked striking, I knew, but the way people were saying hello while we walked by was frightening. Each and every table we passed said something to us, bidding us a hello or nodding one as we passed. Finally I figured out that Samantha was behind me smiling at each and every one of them. She was something else.

As I got to the restroom door, I looked behind us and pulled her in with me. The room was big, but it was one of the kinds that you could actually have privacy in. It had a door lock and one stall, so that we were not going to be interrupted by anyone. I reached behind her and locked the door and stood as close as I could get to her, as I hiked up my skirt and whipped off my panties in one motion. My shoes popping off my feet as I lifted each one to get the other items off. She was not smiling anymore. She had a hungry look in her eyes as she grabbed me and her lips came crashing down on mine.

She pressed me up against the wall, knocking over a small wastebasket that was there. My hands flew to the wall to catch me, to help retain my balance. She was giving me no mercy; she threw her leg between mine, my skirt rising with her thigh until it touched me. The moans that I had wanted to let out at the table came out now, barely audible from the kiss. Her hand moved to my breast and pushed hard, immediately calling my nipple to attention. My back was chilled by the cold wall, making it all the more tantalizing having her against my front, warm, hot even as she pushed at me.

We had hit the wall with a thud that probably the whole restaurant heard, but we didn't care. My hands went to her dress and pulled and gathered until I had her dress up over her hips and had my hands on the back of her thighs pulling her on my lap as I leaned against the wall. She moved her hips against mine; she was pushing and moaning into my lips. I was kissing her and caressing her legs, my hands roaming up and back. I ran one hand up the back of her thigh feeling her stockings against my palms, making me sweat even more. I wished I could lay her down and make her scream. But she had screamed so loudly the night prior, I was afraid. The whole restaurant would hear. And I was such a good customer.

She brought me back to reality as her hand slid between us, down past my navel and lower. My bare legs were against her stockings, she was moving her hips against mine, my hands had found her; I ripped a hole in her hose to get to her, and my hand was now wet with her. My mind raced back to where her hand was going, I could feel it between us. I thought she was going to touch me, my skirt was up and I was shamelessly awaiting her touch. I was touching her and wanted her to touch me. I wanted her badly. Then I realized her finger had just touched my hand that was touching her, she was helping me!!! I nearly exploded right then.

I covered her lips with mine as she started to scream, her moans running together, no longer at intervals. I was holding her on me as best as I could, but she was beginning to flail about, and it was driving me insane. Her skirt was caught on my belt and I heard it rip. She buried her head in my shoulder as she started to orgasm and her arms flew around my neck to hold me as her body shook. I shook with her, just from the excitement of her. We held each other, trying to be quiet. She slid down my legs as I leaned heavily against the wall.

"Oh My God, Abby!" She sounded frightened and I looked at her.

"What Samantha? Are you okay?" I said.

She looked down and on the floor were my panties and her dress was ripped about four inches up the bottom seam. We began laughing. We were children again, caught in mischief. What were we going to do?

As soon as I got my legs back underneath me, I picked up my panties and shoes. I unhooked the panties from one of the shoes and tossed them in the trashcan.

"Thanks Samantha, that was my favorite pair of panties."

She just laughed. She put her hands on my back and kissed me softly and said, "I am sorry."

Then we looked at her skirt. It had ripped cleanly. There was no way we could hide it. The material of her dress was cotton, but it was heavy. You could tell that it was torn. I couldn't think of anything to do. Nothing came to mind at all. Then it occurred to me. "The wait-station. Gerard!!! Come on baby, I have an idea, " I said as I put on my shoes.

She looked as if she could cry on one hand and break into laughter on the other. One look in the mirror, we shared it quickly, we straightened our hair and removed lipstick that was smudged and kissed lightly and went to the door. Deep breath, I opened the door, to my surprise no one was waiting outside. We left and I walked right up to the wait station, grabbed Gerard's hand in mid-sentence with a waiter and pulled him with us into the Foyer.

"I need your help, please," my eyes plead with him as I spoke.

I reached down and showed him Sammie's dress and he began laughing. His laughter rang through the lobby and half of the quiet restaurant. I was blushing profusely; Samantha had darted behind me so that no one could see her torn skirt.

"Was that you in the bathroom making all that noise?" He was bellowing.

I was now mortified. He quieted down some and leaned to us, as if to whisper, but in a moderate voice said, "I hope you had fun in there. And, I am teasing, no one heard much."

He bellowed with laughter again. He then went behind his desk station and came back quickly. He knelt down and stapled Samantha's dress back together.

I rolled my eyes, oh great, how stupid could we look? When he was done, he examined it. To my amazement, you couldn't tell that there had been a rip at all. He somehow had hidden the staples and all was well. I looked at my watch. I now wondered how long we had been gone?

We headed back to the table, this time I pulled Sam's chair out for her and we sat down as if nothing had been out of the ordinary. Des and Jenny were eating dessert. They had ordered some elaborate chocolate thing. It was a mound of chocolate. I mean it smelled good from ten feet away, but it was huge. It was every kind of chocolate and then had chocolate sprinkles and chocolate shavings and chocolate whipped cream. I just stared at it. Des took a bite and made as if it were the Grand Marquee of Desserts, pulling the spoon out of her mouth dramatically slow.

Then she looked at Samantha and looked at me, smiled a cheesy smile, licked her lips and said, "Did you have fun in the restroom?"

I loved Desiree. Her blunt ability to crack any silence was fascinating. I laughed and nodded my head as I reached under the table and held Sam's hand again. Des let it drop there. They finished their dessert while we watched, Jenny handing her spoon to Sam and letting her taste. I declined. I had my dessert already and smiled at Samantha. She was beginning to be everything I had not remembered I had wanted.

Gerard came to the table and leaned to speak to me, "Now, Miss Mitchell?"

I nodded my head. I had ordered Samantha's present and it was time to give it to her. When I leaned toward her, Samantha leaned closer to me and I asked her to excuse me for a moment, I would return shortly. She smiled and knew something was up. I touched her cheek as I arose to retrieve her present. Gerard had everything ready for me. The four staff members that he had asked to help were more than appeasing. They were perfect. What good sports. They were all ready.

I had the present on a silver tray, with a bottle of champagne and four glasses and I carried it out, with the waiters behind me, singing Happy Birthday. The whole restaurant stopped to listen as they finished up with, "Happy Birthday dear Samantha. Happy Birthday to you...and many more."

The other patrons clapped and some yelled happy birthday. Samantha got up and bowed and waved and sat back down. That was cute of her. I stood there with the tray, while Gerard opened the champagne and poured for us. On the tray was a gold envelope. I handed the envelope to her and kissed her on the cheek as I whispered happy birthday to her again. We all stood and toasted.

"To love and friendship" Desiree cheered.

We all repeated, "To love and friendship."

Our glasses clinked together and we all sipped from the champagne. It tasted wonderful. I wanted to kiss her so badly. The taste of the champagne on her tongue, I looked at her, tried to tell her what I was thinking without saying it, just by looking at her. She looked at me and opened the gift I had given her. Inside the envelope were two tickets to the Bahamas, on a Caribbean Cruise Line.

The tickets were for Dec. 28th through Jan 4th. She looked at me, amazed. She held them up for Des and Jenny to see and everyone said "wow" in their own little way. She threw her arms around me and hugged me hard. It was so wonderful. She was so affectionate. She leaned her head back and kissed me softly.

Chapter Ten

We left the restaurant, it was nearly nine-thirty now and the gallery was just down the street. We planned to meet the girls in the parking lot of the gallery and I took the bags we had left at the cabin and put them in the trunk. I noticed that the cooler still sounded as if it had ice in it, the fruit would still be good.

We had laughed the whole way to the gallery about the restroom episode. Samantha had admitted she had never done anything like that before. She couldn't believe that they knew what we had done. I had assured her they knew nothing, it was like Des to assume and try and assume correctly, but that she knew nothing. She was just teasing us.

The gallery was amidst the "gay section" of the city, so we could walk hand-in-hand and not standout. I had a hold of Samantha's hand and Desiree had Jenny's, Des put her arm around me. The four of us walked into the gallery just like that.

We got inside and the party had already begun. Greetings were classic. Jenny became the Diva of Art. She double kissed everyone's cheeks.

I whispered to Sam, "We've met so many people; I can't remember half their names. I do recognize many prominent lesbian and gay figures though. We're in a very elite crowd, that's for sure." I said

There was a singer of national magnitude, whom I had always admired. Her and her wife were wonderful, Samantha talked to them for the most part, while I took the chance to mingle a bit. Des introduced me to her partner; they had a law firm together prior to her fame and fortune in the political realm. We met two art critics, who were so funny. All they did was tell jokes, I had no idea how they were paying attention to the new works. And then we met the artist. She was Russian. I think she was the most beautiful woman I had ever seen, with the exception of Samantha. They had similar features; only Tabrai's hair was longer. Samantha looked at her with amazement. They could have only been a couple of years apart in age, if that. They definitely could have been sisters.

I watched Samantha watch Tabrai; there was something eerie about it. Des elbowed me and motioned toward Samantha as if she noticed too. I shrugged as to why and Des understood. After Tabrai spoke a few words about the pieces, she went off to a reception room, where Jenny had planned a private party. Des scooped us up and pulled us in the room too. There were only ten or twelve people allowed in the room.

Tabrai was shy and it seemed to suit her in here, rather than in the large gallery showroom. She introduced herself to us; we seemed to be the only ones in the room she did not know. Her English was perfect. I hadn't noticed before, but she seemed to not have much of a Russian accent. She first came to me and then to Samantha. When she got to Samantha, they seemed to stare at each other. They didn't say anything, just shook hands and stood there.

Finally Tabrai said, "You look so familiar to me. But, I can't place you."

Samantha didn't say anything, just smiled a shy smile. It was different than any smile I had seen from her. She reached for my hand as she stood there, they spoke idle chitchat and Des was talking to me about the sculptures that were present; I wasn't paying attention to Des. But, rather, I was watching Samantha as she nestled up in my arm and continued to listen to Tabrai.

About ten minutes later, she whispered up to me, "Can we go home now, Abby?" She leaned up her face so that I could see her eyes and she looked tired.

"Sure Sam, anytime." I said.

She moved around me and said goodbye to Des and they gave each other hugs. Des kissed me on the cheek and said,

"She's a winner, don't let her go." From Des, that was a huge compliment.

We moved over to where Jenny was talking to the other group of people and Jenny hugged us both with great enthusiasm.

We said goodbye and she said that she had a great time at dinner and winked at me and said, "I especially liked the thumping sound from the bathroom."

We both dropped our jaws. Jenny was giggling with delight and she hugged us both again.

"Could you really hear?" I asked.

Jenny shook her head yes as she laughed even louder. With that, we turned and walked out of the party, I don't know which of us was more embarrassed?

⚜

We drove home in light conversation, her head against my shoulder as she searched for a music station. She had stopped the CD player and moved it to radio. Some soft music without words came on and she stopped there.

"Did you have a good time?" I asked her.

"I have never had a birthday this nice before. For some reason, most of my birthdays have turned out either really boring, work or something, or they were disasters. This one was perfect, you made it perfect." she was smiling. "I can't believe how spontaneous you are. You just do the most pleasant things for me. I watched you for so long wondering what you were like. You are so much better than I even envisioned. I knew you would be soft and secure, intriguing and intelligent, I even thought you would be spontaneous.... But, I never knew it could be like this. You bought us tickets to the Bahamas. You have made my birthday an occasion to remember. Thank You, Abigail."

She leaned up and kissed my cheek and snuggled back into my arm. The rest of the drive was quiet. I felt so at home with Samantha.

As we turned to go to Sam's house, she asked me, "Can you

take me to your house? I have driven by thousands of times, trying to see if you were home, but never been there. I'd like to see it, if you don't mind. I don't feel like going home."

I was a little startled by her request. I had been with her for the last forty-some hours and felt so at home, it was like the rest of my life wasn't even there.

"I'd like that too." I kissed the top of her head, passed her house and headed towards mine.

We pulled into my driveway. For the first time, practically since I had bought the house, I took good look at it. I felt insecure. I loved her house so much; hers was just what I had always liked; it was perfect. And, now as I looked at mine, I wanted it to be as peaceful and homey as hers. I looked at her as she looked at my house, hoping and praying she would like it. For some reason, that was important.

The outside of my house was white, with pine trim on the shutters, with a large bay window, in which sat my breakfast nook.

I said to her, "Underneath that window is a window box. My neighbor, Beulah, planted flowers in it and keeps them up for me. I've caught her a number of times watering them when I come home from work. She takes care of my yard and my cat when I leave for the weekend or holidays."

My porch was only 12' long and all wooden. I had two padded lawn lounge chairs on it with green and cream stripes. They were full and fit the wood frames and then some. A small white wooden table sat between them. I'd wished many a night that someone would sit outside with me, but the truth be known, I'd never even sat outside with anyone other than myself. I had a porch swing on the other end of the porch, just to the left of the stairs.

As we climbed the stairs, she had said nothing. I took her hand and looked for my house key, I had not turned on the porch light before I left. Samantha pulled me towards the porch swing.

"I want to swing," she stated.

I laughed, "Your wish is my command birthday girl."

It was late at this point and I didn't know that any of my neighbors were even up, so I let her sit down and I knelt between her legs, my waist resting between her thighs. I put my hands on her calves and lifted her skirt enough to slide my hands up her inner thighs and began massaging. She leaned back in the seat. She couldn't swing, because I was in the way.

I ran my hands down her outer thighs and leaned forward and placed my head on her chest. She held my head to her bosom as I continued to massage. I inhaled her scent as I inched my hands slowly up her thighs almost touching her panties, but moving back down as she tensed up. She kissed my head as she ran her hands through my hair, lacing her fingers through tendrils and moving down. She moved her hands to just below my ears and lifted my face to hers and brushed her lips against mine, tenderly.

"I love you, Abby," she whispered and kissed me again.

I started to tell her the same as her lips tore into mine, pulling me up off my knees and bringing me to her, her arms now around my waist as her hips slid forward to mine. My words were lost in that kiss.

We kissed for a while and then she moved her lips down my face to my earlobe, "Abby, take me inside and make love to me, please?"

I gathered myself together and tried to find my keys again. I had dropped them in the heat of the moment on the porch. I found them and somehow found the house key.

As I unlocked the door, her hands sought me from behind, caressing my breasts; I could feel her breath on my neck. The door fell open finally and Chloe, my cat came running forward, stopping in mid-flight when she saw a stranger with me and headed back towards the bedroom, her safety. I couldn't even get the light switch flipped before Samantha had my lips again, attached to hers in a passionate exchange. Her hands were moving gracefully behind me unbuttoning and unzipping my skirt and dropping it over my hips as I tried to shut the door.

I fumbled with the lock and finally got it shut and secure. My blouse was half unbuttoned before I could even get a chance at getting her dress unzipped in back. Hers was easy though, it unzipped from the top nearly to the waist and I pulled it off her shoulders and in an instant, as I undid the belt on her waist, it fell in one movement to the floor. My blouse was off as soon as I pulled my arms through it and fell also. We embraced again, this time I felt her skin next to mine and remembered the first time we made love. I couldn't get enough of her kiss; her lips were making me needy.

"I don't want to make love right now," Samantha's voice was husky.

She kissed me more, fully and passionately. Her hands continued to leave a trail of heat on my back and sides, never stopping in one place.

My right hand was caressing her breast, rolling her nipple in my fingers as I whispered back, "Why not?"

She pressed herself against me as she began to speak, "I want to make love to you with my mind tonight, here in your house, I want to make it mine. I want to get acquainted with you and your world like you did with mine; leaving out the physical exchange and replacing it with a mental note as we did the other night, ending with us sleeping in each other's arms. Is that okay with you?"

I couldn't be more pleased. I was exhausted from the weekend, my body not used to the reactions she was pulling forth. I loved listening to her voice and wanted to delve into her world as much as she wanted to be in mine. I ran my tongue over her lips quickly and down her neck; I slid her bra strap off her shoulder with one finger and my tongue continued its trek to her nipple as I replaced my fingers with my lips.

Her intake of breath was raspy as I sucked lightly and said finally, "I would like that."

I took her hands in mine and removed my mouth from her breast, reluctantly.

"Let me show you my house." I said.

We walked to where the light switch was and I turned it once, dim lights came on in my living room, the two of us, almost naked, explored the room. I had one couch, an oversized camel colored leather. I loved the sound of sitting on it, the squish of the leather as you settled. It had two navy throw pillows and a cream throw over the back. On each side of the couch, which sat directly in front of the fireplace, there were cherry end tables, long and sleek. The couch was unusually high and the tables accentuated its height beautifully. There were brass lamps with navy hoods on the tables and various magazines and each had a coaster from Kansas State University, where I graduated with my Master's. That was the center of my room.

I had hard wood floors and the couch sat on an oriental rug. When you walked in the door, you were directly in the middle of the room, on the left, in the corner, was a "V" bookshelf full of literature and magazines. Following that, in the next corner of the room was a reading chair. It matched the leather of the couch and was accented with a tall cherry lamp table that had a magazine rack on the bottom. The mantle of the fireplace held my awards from years gone by, various athletic awards from college and a couple of marketing awards from the company. In the middle were my two regional softball MVP trophies, my favorites.

She touched my awards, each one, "You are a very talented lady."

"That was a long time ago..." I said.

On the right of the fireplace was my entertainment center, cherry again, and then another bookshelf. On the opposite wall hung an original piece of art, lit, that had been in our family for a very long time.

"I don't spend much time in this room, it makes me feel lonely for some reason." I said.

She looked closely at the painting, "This is an original, isn't it? It's magnificent.

"Yes, I admired it greatly as a child and grandmother gave it to me a couple years ago, she had said she wanted to see me enjoy it before she died; she's still living." I said.

I led Sam into the next part of the house. We went into the hallway and off to the right, I ignored the door, it was my bedroom, we would come back to it.

Down the hallway on the left was my kitchen, where Chloe was waiting to be fed.

"Let me feed Chloe. Do you want to see if there is something to snack on in the fridge? I am hungry again." I crinkled my nose at being such a pig, but I was starving.

"Will this work?" She held up some crackers and cheese.

"Perfect." I said as I grabbed a bottle of wine, two glasses and corkscrew.

"Oh, God, Sam. I completely forgot about work tomorrow. I have a presentation at ten o'clock and I have to tell the officers what I'm going to do, which is going to require a letter of resignation." I looked at her with a crease in my forehead. I hadn't felt tension this entire weekend until just that moment.

"Well, what do we need to do to get you ready? I'm sure I can help. How far are you on the presentation? And, what do you need me to do?" She asked.

"Oh, don't you look the corporate executive in your bra and panties?" I said. She had gotten so serious all of the sudden. "You could take the corporate world by storm, I'm sure." I teased. I was rolling with laughter. "I'm picturing you the presentation room with the clients in your bra and panties." I went to her to kiss away her pout. Her bottom lip had flown out and looked as if a bird could perch there for life.

"Awwww, honey, did I hurt your feelings?" I said.

"No," she pouted.

She was playing this up I realized and I must let her have her game. I moved toward her and placed my hands on her waist. I gathered her next to me and embraced her tightly.

She said, "That's all I wanted, a hug."

"Okay, let me think a minute. We can do this. My presentation is done, all but the last set of graphics and I have to do that on the computer. I have to finish it, even though I am leaving. I did promise my client. My letter of resignation...can you do that?"

She replied with glee, "I would love to tell them that you are leaving and coming to me."

"Okay, let's get to it," I said with a peck.

I helped her gather the snack tray and wine and we moved into the hallway again. We moved to the left, to the back of the house, past the two guest bedrooms and the utility room, past the library and stereo room and into the last room on the right, my office.

"It's like walking into a different world, the difference in this room and the others." She said.

I had a marble desk, gray and black with a black top. It was huge. It filled most of the room. There was a stereo and bookshelves with numerous books on marketing, advertising, management, time management, etc. The carpeting was navy and the walls were cream with a navy stripe at the top about four inches tall. There was a lone pillar in the corner, in front of the desk, that held a statue of a woman, standing proud and tall on four steps, holding a book and wearing a gold medallion. The wall adjacent the door held two, six drawer, wooden file cabinets. I moved to the desk and pulled out the black leather executive chair and laid the wine and glasses down. I motioned her to lay her contents down nearby.

"This is my haven. What do you think?" as I spread my arms around the room.

She walked around the desk to where I was standing, "This is how you think isn't it? Sharp and concise, yet practical and soothing?"

I had never heard it put that way before, she was always analyzing. "I guess it is..." I said. "I feel pretty 'at home' here-more than anywhere else."

I started to pull out my laptop computer that I used at home as she opened the wine and poured both glasses. She handed one to me and sipped comfortably from hers. I turned on my computer and waited for my programs to install as she walked over to the sculpture on the pillar.

She examined it from the angles she could reach and finally asked, "whose is this?"

"Mine." I replied.

"You did this?" she turned to face me, her face showing her surprise.

I nodded in affirmation. I had done it the year prior, it was very rough, but had raw appeal, definitely done by an amateur.

"Tell me about her. She is standing for more than liberty and justice, isn't she?"

She had seen that I had gone for a Lady of Liberty type motive, but, by far, had surpassed it in the woman's meaning. As I began to work on the graphics for the rest of the presentation, I spoke to her about the statue. She perched on the desk, grabbed a pen and paper and began to write my letter of resignation, while she listened.

I began to tell her, "The statue is representative of my success. The book is a Bible, which has given me the strength and wisdom to surpass the ordinary and extraordinary things that have happened in my life. The torn and tattered dress that she wears, which can only be seen if you are really looking and in good light, is symbolic of the way we can smooth away scars. We literally hide them, well, they are mostly hidden to the regular bystander, but if examined they are there. The lack of shoes and jewelry is a representation of her lack of materialistic nature. She needs nothing to survive other than the book and herself. And, finally, the four stairs are the Olympic stairs plus one. She's not only trained for an athletic event, but life itself." I looked up momentarily to see if she was listening and she was, while she wrote, a cracker resting on her lips. I continued, "Her gold medallion doesn't say first place, but rather is made of pure gold and has been purified by the fire. It's smooth and clean, the outer lines crisp in the philosophic refinement, just as her life has become."

Neither of us spoke. Intermittently, she would take a cracker and cheese and whatever else fancied her for that bite and feed us, through our work. I loved the way this woman took care of business.

We sipped on our wine and ate our snacks.

Finishing the story, I dodged the questioning eyes that were certain to be there. I had just explained the pain and triumph in my life that would next have to be explained by events. I knew that.

Instead, the woman of my dreams, as she was unfolding, said, "Did you see the angel over my fireplace?"

"No, I didn't." I said.

"The next time we go into my house, look at the angel over the fireplace. She's a gift from my mother," She said slowly and quietly.

This was the first I remembered her really speaking of any family members.

"Mother died when I was fifteen, at the hand of my father. She'd given it to me for my fifteenth birthday, had taken money from the family food fund and purchased it. Abby, she gave it to me in the privacy of the bathroom, because she wasn't allowed to spend money on me." She said and stopped.

As she slid the pen across the paper in a final gesture, she laid the pad down and put her elbows on her knees. I looked only briefly and smiled, I didn't want to have her stop talking. I wanted to know about her.

I thought to myself how dastardly could a child's life be? Her father killed her mother? Good Lord!!!

She spoke again, "I was an only child and my family was wealthy. My father worked for one of the largest investment firms in Charlotte, the banking capital of the nation at that time, and we lived well. Yet, my mother was not allowed to spend money and was divvied a budget for the house. She ran our household on less than I run the shelter, and we had a staff. Look at her and see what I have left of my mother sometime. She is beautiful, as was my mother." Samantha spoke in the most southern accent I had ever heard when she had told her story.

I looked at her and it was as if she had become a child. Her eyes were misty as she remembered her mother. I thought she was done, but Samantha continued her story.

She moved her bare feet to where they were laying in my lap, her legs over the arm of my chair as I typed and moved the graphics where I needed them.

"I was adopted from Russia. My parents weren't able to have children, because my mother had to have an emergency hysterectomy after my father beat her so badly that he ruptured something inside her. And, because of the social status of having a child, my father had 'allowed' my mother to adopt. My mother had told me that night, on my birthday how much she had wanted a child and how much she loved me..."

The tears were once again streaming down her face, but this time I let her be. I let her continue the story as I worked, not paying attention to what I was doing, but to her story.

"She loved me so much, I always felt that. My father, the bastard, never touched me. She would have killed him. I had been adopted she told me the night of my fifteenth birthday. Something that was amazing to me, because I hadn't known. No one had that I knew of...but she told me the name of my mother in Russia and that she had met her when they went there to pick me up. It was against the rules, but that because my family was so wealthy, they had paid to be able to do so. My mother wanted to know my birthmother, so she could tell me about her later. My birth mother was beautiful she said, looked a lot like I did, and I should be proud to have a woman love me so much as to make a better life for me in America."

Immediately my mind went back to the gallery and how she had stared at Tabrai. They had a striking resemblance. An eerie chill ran through my body. Tabrai was from Russia too and they could be sisters in stature and looks alone.

Samantha's story continued, "I have no real recollection of what happened the night my mother died. My father found the angel in my room later apparently; he used to scour my room for anything to complain about and question me. He brought it to me in my room one night and began drilling me. I told him it was a gift from a friend for my birthday. He was not satisfied with that and he started to throw it. I grabbed his hand and yanked it free somehow. He hit me, knocked me out I guess? I woke up and my mother was dead. She must have stopped him. I don't know. The police were there and they scooted me out the door to the hospital for the night after a doctor checked me out. I stayed there until my grandmother could come and get me, two days later. She finished raising me." She looked at me until I met her gaze.

I leaned back in my chair, I had finished the graphics, the presentation was ready, and I was ready to comfort my loving friend. I pulled her into my lap from the desktop and held her like a baby, while I rocked back and forth in the chair. There were no more tears from Sammie over the story; however, she looked at me with intensity, but no tears.

I asked her, "Are you healed?"

She understood. "Yeah, I am. It took along time, but I am. I let go of my mother about three years ago. Let her get on, because I had the strength to do alone, finally. What about you? Are you healed Abby?"

I thought for a moment and answered, "I am healed from my past, with the exception of the relationship I had prior to this. And, only time will tell, if my grieving process is complete." I knew I had answered truthfully. I had only time to tell how I would respond to Samantha, as a measure as to whether or not I was really healed.

Samantha and I had talked the weekend before about my life and what I had been through. For the most part, the nine deaths in eight years were the roughest part of it. I had also had an abusive relationship. It was for that alone, that I gave time to the crisis center and I knew that Samantha and I had been in the same situation. It was strange that she had been in one coming from an abusive home; the patterns we followed were scary at times.

"Samantha," I spoke into her eyes, "I'm learning about you. I find strength in your words and wisdom in your manner. I'm glad that I decided to take the position at the shelter. I want to help you fight. You fight for your mother, right?"

She took her arms, which were folded up around her as I held her, and wrapped them around me, "Yes. I fight for my mother and the women like her that were not fortunate enough, as we were, to get out."

I did not kiss her at this time. I had no desire. I held my new friend; I held her close. I had given something to Samantha that was more near and dear to me than anything else, and I didn't even know if she knew it, for her birthday that night, Samantha had acquired my heart.

Chapter Eleven

The Spanish Acquisition had to have been easier than turning in my letter of resignation that day. It was Monday morning and the office was a wreck. I had gotten up that morning to Samantha; I smiled to myself at the thought. We had each showered, she had typed my letter and jetted out the door to her house to dress. We had slept so peacefully in each other's arms the night before that I felt rested and vibrant.

The office was erratic and I was losing my cool. I had gone into the office and laid my letter of resignation down on the desk for the key officer as my answer to their question of my retirement fund. In the letter it spelled out what I wanted done and how I had intended to do it and that my last day on the job was October First.

Sam had done an excellent job on the letter; I hadn't a change to make on it. My morning had consisted of going to the office; I had my secretary proof the plans for the proposal, made the meeting, and been a huge success.

I had intended to meet Samantha for lunch downtown at an old secluded place she knew of, but I had received an urgent message that the board wanted to see me. I had called and we had rescheduled for an hour later, which actually worked out better for both of us anyway and I headed for the meeting room.

What could these jerks possibly want? I had spelled it out for them. Once I reached the meeting room, the key officer had taken the meeting to order and selected me to pick on. There were all eleven of us present that were "invited" to join in the endeavor. I was the last to sign; everyone knew it, no big shock.

The key officer, Reginald Porter, suggested, "Miss Mitchell might not, after all this time, be fit for this type of work."

I was taken aback.

He then went on to deny any of my success in the firm and to put down my biggest proposals and suggest that I was removed from the presentation package that had been submitted that morning after my proposal to our new client.

I sat there and listened to what Mr. Porter said, I soaked up every word. I thought about Samantha. What would she do if this were a crisis at the shelter? I had three things to think of: My future in this business, my reputation he was shredding at the moment, and what would happen if I got fired right now? My future in the business was actually pretty sound. I could get client letters and I had been offered three jobs with other firms in the last year. I should be okay. Someone else had to know that these guys were crooked.

My reputation, however, I was worried about. I had worked with these people for seven years. I think it was high time I stood up for myself. What if I got fired right then? I had to think. Would I lose my retirement if I was fired right then? I remembered hearing that I would not be granted the retirement program if I left the firm of my own will or that I had been proven to break company policy or procedure. I needed help here a second, I was unclear about that and I didn't want to react in a rash manner.

Mr. Porter continued to pluck feathers from what appeared to be my solid reputation, with a barrage of lies and slurs. I had an idea. I reached for my pager making sure that no one saw me; I turned it off and back on. It went off as if it were receiving a page. Mr. Porter was more than annoyed, but excused me while I placed the call. The phone was in the adjoining office and I went inside it and called Desiree's office.

The secretary put me through immediately, as I prayed Desiree would be in. It was the lunch hour and I had no idea if Des would be there or not. Thank God, she was in.

Desiree answered, "To what do I owe this pleasure, Abby?"

I had no time to waste; I filled Desiree in immediately. She gave me the advice I needed.

I told her, " I owe you on this one."

She had great advice and told me that she had just written a client retention agreement between her and I, in the event that they asked if I had legal representation, to give them her partner's name, Julia Francis-Harding as my representing attorney.

Julia was ruthless, one of the most renowned lesbian attorney's in the country and I was pleased with that. "Thank you, Desiree. Gotta go. Bye."

I hung up and ran by my office before returning to the meeting. As Mr. Porter started in, explaining that because of my lack of effort in supporting the project that they would be unable to have enough funds available for the proposed project unless everyone took a 3% cut in pay.

"What?" Jean Neuman burst out with. "I can't afford a cut in pay, I have a family to provide for." She was livid and turned immediately to me.

The whole room was buzzing. Mr. Porter eying me keenly, knowing he placed me in just the position he wished for maximum effect.

They must have anticipated this move by me and had already drawn up contracts and were passing them out to everyone but me.

As my fellow employees were reading their contracts for their pay cuts, I placed the folder I had retrieved from my office on the table. Mr. Porter looked at me inquisitively.

"Is there something you want to say, Miss Mitchell?" He asked.

I had the opportunity I needed. I handed the folder to Johnson, who was sitting next to me, a fellow employee.

I began my quest, "Yes, Mr. Porter, there is."

I then began to address the room; "I have been working on numbers from the reports given us by the Officers. I have found a $3.2 million dollar flaw in the plan. Because of this, I have elected not to participate, to roll my retirement account over to an IRA and I have turned in my letter of resignation."

Mr. Porter was furious; his face was flushed. "I hope you are aware of a huge infraction here, and the possibility of a lawsuit?" He said. "Are you prepared to back up such malicious accusations about *MY* company?"

I, along with the others, caught the word "my" company and not ours any longer.

"Yes, Sir, I am." I replied.

"Well, you can't possibly have brought this forward yourself, so be prepared to hear from our attorney's. You are fired Miss Mitchell." He had said the magic words.

"I believe that you will be hearing from my attorney, Mr. Porter, Julia Francis-Harding." I let her name ring out in the room.

She was very well known for representing lesbians and I knew that, but I also knew her reputation for chewing people up and spitting them out. She had the highest win ratio of cases of any attorney in the county. There had been an article recently in the newspaper about her success. I am sure Desiree planted it for the value of the re-election, but it had been quite informative. I had not intended to sue the company or anything else for that matter. Desiree wanted me to get fired, because then she could write them a letter threatening them to take my retirement. We figured that they couldn't take anyone else's money, if I showed the report and I was leaving anyway. I loved Desiree.

I left the room immediately, without waiting to hear anything further. Mr. Porter was babbling as I walked out the door. The room was buzzing even more than when I tossed the report to Johnson.

I went to my office and caught a look at the time. I gathered my personal items, which fit in a box that my secretary had gotten for me and she helped me out to the elevator with the items. She was crying.

"It's okay, Tamara. It'll be fine, I promise. This is for the best. You take care of yourself." I hugged her and left. I liked her a lot. She had been awarded to me for attaining an account that everyone thought was impossible and she had made my life much easier. But, she had to stay, because she was a single mother and needed the money.

Something about leaving was good. I had been here so long and hadn't realized how much effort I put into going nowhere. I really was about to take a stab at making my life what I wanted, not what I could tolerate. It was going to be interesting.

❧

I arrived at the restaurant a little later than I intended, because I had to gather my things and all; Samantha had already ordered and finished her lunch. She was reading when I caught sight of her. On cue, she turned to find me watching her. I stood across the room and just gazed at her. Her extreme beauty still took me by surprise each time I looked at her and remembered that she loved me. Someone like her loved me?

I tipped my chin to her from across the room and winked the sexiest wink I could muster. I motioned with my head to the restroom door, a few feet from me. I watched her break into a grin. She was giggling visibly as she motioned for me to come to her with her finger in that wicked way that made me know she wanted me there now. I walked slowly to the table. I wasn't self-conscious in the gray pantsuit and jacket I had on. The cut fit me perfectly. I had a seamstress that I had found in town copy a suit I had purchased in all different materials and colors. I had about twenty suits just like this one, the only differences other than color and material was small variations in the jacket. I got about two tables away from her and stopped.

I placed my index finger on my chest and mouthed, "YOU want ME," and pointed to the table, "there?"

She laughed again and nodded. She raised one brow and mouthed back to me, "NOW!"

Now I laughed as I reached the table, bent to her and whispered, "I sure hope you like me a lot, because I am now all yours, I just got fired."

With that I sat down across the table from her.

She didn't waste a moment, "Why?"

I filled her in on all the details, including the one that had me clearing her schedule for the day. I knew we had work to do before I was allowed to begin work with her.

"Consider this your interview, Darling," she said.

She motioned to the waitress and within moments I had a meal delivered in front of me and I began eating. I was starving again. All this fun with her was making me hungry all the time. I used to forget to eat, but lately found myself enjoying it again. We talked the entire hour we spent at the restaurant about what we had to do in order to get me fully prepared to take the position. The first priority was getting me situated in the office of Samantha's friend. While I ate, she called Monica and asked if she could see us this afternoon. Samantha reached for her planner, in her purse, jotted something down and hung up. She then cleared her whole afternoon with Miranda and we were ready.

"Sweetie, she can see us at three o'clock, we have an hour. I need to call for a board meeting for Wednesday night," she was jotting again in the planner, "and, I need to get the job description and paperwork for you. You must fill it out prior."

I nodded in agreement.

"We should be set," she said. "I thought you might get a kick out of this; I went home this morning to dress to find a ton of messages from the staff. Miranda was the worst. She was in charge yesterday at the shelter and it must have been a slow night, because she took every chance to call the house. Her messages got more irate as the night progressed until around midnight, when she finally admitted to giving up and promising that she would corner me this morning." Samantha's eyes were brilliant as she spoke. The light coming in the window hit them just right and they were ablaze.

I got lost watching her. She was animated as she spoke of the shelter.

She continued, "There is a new woman at the shelter. She is

so depressed and possibly beyond our realm of help. I really am not sure what to do with her."

I took my last bite and pushed my plate to the side. I couldn't concentrate on what Sam continued to say, but was mesmerized with her appearance.

She had on a teal and cream business suit. The waistcoat was cut and fitted, with matching cloth buttons. It showed a cream shell that she wore underneath and I wondered what color of bra she had on. She spoke in the background while I watched her and noticed intricate details in her mannerisms. Her skirt was also fitted and I knew that it would show her curves. I had seen her in this outfit before. Her shoes were a cream and teal combination, contrasting perfectly and she had a fuscia hankie in her left breast pocket. It was a smart suit. Her hair was up in a French knot and had one ringlet that fell near her right ear. Gold hoop earrings and her new necklace I had purchased were her only accessories other than her rings. She was so beautiful.

As I gazed at her, I realized she had asked me something and was waiting for an answer.

"I am sorry, Darling, I was staring at you and noticing what you were wearing and your voice just lulled me into a trance. I didn't hear what you said."

She smiled, "I just noticed you watching me and you were staring, sort of off in space. 'What were you thinking?' is what I asked." She drawled.

"Mmmmm your voice, Samantha. You're dangerous. I was actually wondering what color of bra you had on under that suit, but I don't want you to tell me, because I would like to be surprised later." I grinned as I spoke.

She blushed lightly, "And so you shall," she said in her best southern accent.

It sent a chill from my midsection to my collarbone.

She looked at her watch, "We must be going or we'll be late meeting Monica."

I nodded in agreement and called the waitress. Sam picked

up the check and we were off. Once we were out the door, she walked as close as she could get to me.

"Abby, can we ride together? Let's drop my truck off at the house...okay?"

I agreed to follow her and we each got into separate vehicles and departed. I played the radio on the drive, singing along at the top of my lungs, feeling free and clear of the problems that had persisted at work. Finally they would be gone. So would most of my income, but at least it would be worth it.

I pulled into Samantha's driveway behind her Rodeo and she motioned me into the house with her. I cut my ignition and climbed out of the Mazda. Inside the door, I was attacked. She slammed herself against me and I met her lips with mine. Her lips tasted like cinnamon. Her hand went immediately to my breast and I was immediately engaged in full body reaction. She walked slowly backwards as we kissed, leading me all the way through her house to the bedroom, groping and kissing. We had less than an hour before we had to be at the appointment with Monica.

What was she thinking? Was I the only rational person here? I laughed at the thought, ME RATIONAL around Samantha? Never.

She undressed me with skill and confidence and laid me down on the bed, my legs hanging over and my feet still touching the floor. I grabbed pillows to tuck behind my head as I watched her walk around to her night stand and switch on the CD player. No words, only strings again, whispering strings. The music was slow and sweet. She began moving back towards me and she slid out of her garments, careful to lay them aside, as she had mine, for re-entry later. She stood in front of me in a teal bra and panties. I now had my question answered. It was lace and very thin. I wanted to touch. I leaned forward, but she held up her hand and said no without saying a word.

She began to dance as the music thickened...slowly swaying as she moved toward me. I lay back against the pillow and watched her. She got so close to me that I could feel her legs almost touch mine. Placing her hands on each side of my waist, she began to inch toward my lips. She got to a point that she was almost touching them and she began to trail her lips downward, never touching me, but close enough I could feel her. My body anticipated her every movement. In the few moments that she teased me, my body became more alive, more vibrant. She pulled something out of her hair and it fell out of the French knot.

All of the sudden, she put one foot against mine and her hand went to my inner thigh. Her other foot moved with her hand to part my legs. She ran her hair down my stomach as she kissed my body, and slid my panties aside and made love to me.

It didn't take long for her to please me, bringing my body to climax. I was unaware of just how loud I was. She moved to lie upon me, to hold me and whisper to me how much she loved me as I shuddered in her arms. I shook and quivered as she stroked my hair and embraced me tenderly.

As I calmed down, my eyes fixed on hers. My eyes said what I couldn't; 'I love you'. I wrapped my arms around her, unable to move; motionless with the exception of the remaining shudders that still ensued.

As soon as I got an exchange of energy; I rolled her so that she was on her stomach. I had caught her off guard, so it had been easy. I placed my body on hers and began to caress her breasts underneath her, reaching around.

I spoke to her as my hands moved on her body, making love to her. "You were so beautiful at lunch, your hair was perfect, made me want to wrap my finger in that ringlet." I kissed her hair, pulling lightly with my lips. "It made me want to touch it...your eyes sparkled with the light from the window. I could have devoured you at any moment. Do you know I think of your touch and quiver all times of the day, with or without you around?"

I moaned loudly in her ear as I touched her for the first time, my hips grinding against hers moving my hand. As she began to become more audible, I became less talkative and paid attention to her movement. I let her lead me and found her shuddering almost immediately. She reached around and pulled me closer to her as she shook. She kept saying my name over and over as she got louder. It was making me drip on her. She made me feel like no one else had before. She shook underneath me and I held her close to me, moving so that I lay next to her as she moved to her side so that we could cuddle. We held each other and kissed; she expressed herself in her kisses. Each one had meaning and I was beginning to be able to tell the difference.

I could see the time on her alarm clock on the nightstand. I whispered to her, "Honey, it's ten to three."

All I wanted to do was fall asleep here, like this, with her. But, we got up and dressed quickly. I helped her put her hair back in the knot and we flew out the door.

In the car she held my hand again. That was almost my favorite. She was affectionate and attentive, something I had missed out on in my last relationship. We were ten minutes late to the appointment, not something either of us was used to. Monica was still in with another client, so we finished the discussion we had started in the car about my placement in Monica's office.

The meeting went smoothly and we left with all the plans that had me in the office on Wednesday morning at nine o'clock. We were officially merged. I was now the Director Of Fundraising and Marketing for the shelter. We decided to celebrate.

Chapter Twelve

There were more things to celebrate lately than either of us was used to. As we left the office, smiles dawning our faces, we talked about the prospects for the shelter. I was enthralled with her wonder and creativity; she had put a lot of thought into her dream for the shelter. The shelter currently worked on a shoestring budget and couldn't afford proper food for the inhabitants.

She had prepared several reports on the options that might be available to the shelter and offered to show them to me in such a quaint manner, "I'll show you the reports," drawing out her words like a German matron, "and you can select your plan of action."

We both giggled and progressed the conversation as we drove back to my house, so I could check my messages and read my mail.

Once there I said, "We can do a number of things, but I am going to toss this out, I don't want to share you tonight with anyone. I don't want to be in public. Maybe we could just order pizza, listen to music and prepare me for my new position?"

"We could play late..." She said.

It was exciting to just think about that, envisioning it with her as my willing victim. Feeding her this time. I remembered back to our first night together.

She asked me, "What are you thinking about?"

"I was just thinking how it might be fun to feed you and return the favor from Friday night. Can you believe it's only Monday?"

❧

We went into my office to retrieve the necessary supplies: legal pads, pens, paper clips and a stapler. As I picked out the essential supplies, I noticed she was at the statuette again. This time she was touching it.

"Do you like it?" I asked.

"I love it. I can't believe you're so talented, not to put you down in anyway," she smiled, "but, you do so many things so well. What made you make this again? I was so tired the other night, I remember most of it, but I was so mesmerized by your voice, that I think I lost some of it. And, it didn't help that I was trying to write your letter of resignation either," she smiled.

I put the supplies down on the desk and walked to her and put my arms around her from behind.

I explained again, "I made this a year ago. It explains the pain and triumph in my life. I told you about the Bible, the medallion, and the four stairs representing the Olympic stairs plus one…meaning that training in athletics is just a step below training in life and that we all actually train in that respect. She stands on the top in excellence. The torn and tattered dress is full of scars that are smoothed over. You can't see them unless you're really close. It's like when someone gets to know me. I have a great exterior, but inside I am torn, I have had tremendous pain and have scars from it, as does everyone. She is not a materialistic woman, but rather the lack of accessories, even though she is wearing a dress; show the importance of the medallion. The medallion is strong, pure and refined. Samantha, that's me…at my finest. Even though she doesn't quite look like me, she is…or an extension of. And, well, there is some other significance, but it's kind of silly," I said.

I stopped for a moment, because I wasn't sure I had wanted to get any deeper, but Sam sensed that and held me closer to her by grabbing my arms with her left arm and touching the statuette's face with her right hand.

"Abby, why does she have no real facial features?" she asked.

"Well," I continued, "I had a really hard time about five years ago. My girlfriend had broken up with me and I was about at my end. I went to the lake, thought about killing myself and saw this woman...she came to comfort me, an angel, I guess. Anyway, I've never told anyone. She had long dark red hair, and she just held me while I cried. I survived the crisis and met my next girlfriend a few months later."

I spoke softly, "It was the only real thing I could see of this woman. I was pretty torn up. It was like a dream, but yet, it wasn't. She was real to me, I felt her touch."

She leaned to me and kissed my cheek. She spoke even softer than I and in the most alluring southern accent, "Must be why you love *my* hair so much? I notice when we make love that you're always touching my hair in the most tender of ways. You make love to every part of my body. No one has ever done that before. They made love to me, but not like you do. You take my entire being with you. When I'm with you..." she turned to face me, "I feel as if there is no one left in the world but us."

She kissed me intensely, her hands in my hair, pulling me to her fiercely. I joined her kiss with as much enthusiasm.

After she released my lips, she said, "Maybe I remind you of her?" jokingly.

We both laughed softly.

The doorbell rang and we jumped a bit.

"Oh, the pizza is here." I said.

"I'll get it, you finish getting your things in here and I'll take care of Mr. Pizza Boy."

She was so funny. Always had a way of lightening up the situation. I hadn't wanted to tell her about the angel. The angel had saved my life and it was hard to admit that I had needed it. Maybe someday I would tell her, but not just yet. I felt that I could trust her with it, but there was something about the angel that was not to share. I shook the thoughts from my head and got the things we needed.

I headed towards the living room, stopping at the bedroom and changed into a pair of nylon sweats when she found me.

"Here's a pair for you." I tossed her a pair, a little large for her and she changed. I then grabbed big Kansas State University sweatshirts for us both.

After that, we moved back out to the living room and I started a fire, while she selected our music to work by. She suggested a few and together we picked. She put it on random and away we went. We continued to talk about the shelter. I had worked there long enough to know what the problems were, so we settled in on the couch and began working.

We had pizza and I opened a bottle of wine, a Beringer that my friend brought back from Germany for me. We ate and we talked, sipped wine and kissed. We held hands and sang the songs that we knew. It was the most content I'd been in years. I really did feel at home with her.

The room I had avoided for so long came alive for me that night. It became a part of my home that I knew I would cherish, just because it felt like home again. I had spent time as a child in our living room, with the family, watching television or playing games and I had sure missed it. For the first time in about seventeen years, since my father had been killed, I felt like I was part of a family, even though it was just the two of us.

"Abby, what's the matter?" she said sweetly as she touched my hand.

I'd been sitting quiet for some time, remembering my childhood and thinking about how wonderful it felt to be here with her.

"I was just remembering when I was a child. I guess you bring out things in me that I'd forgotten."

I smiled at her and leaned to her slowly, teasing her somewhat, and brushed my lips against hers as lovingly as I could. To change the subject, I asked her how much money the shelter would need to do what she wanted. I had an inkling that she might already know...and she did. She gave me the figure and I began my flowchart of how I would get there.

For the next two hours we figured out our plan of action. When we were done, we went over both our plans. She had engaged in a plan to spend the money that I had planned to get. It really would work. As we went over the final phase, we were both more excited about the shelter than ever before. She laid down her pen and pad and drew her eyes to mine. She moved from the leather couch we had been lounging on to one knee.

As she knelt before me, she took my hand in hers. I watched her quietly. I had no fear in what she was doing. "Abigail, I can't give you anything in this life, but my love. I can't promise you anything but my loyalty, but, I can promise you this, all that I have is yours...now and forever."

An endearing love song came on the stereo; she sang to me and then we made love.

Chapter Thirteen

The next few weeks consisted of furnishing the office and getting to know Monica.. I had so much experience, that moving into the job wasn't too tough. My days were long, about twelve hours being the average. I started work at seven-thirty and so did Sam. We were going back and forth between each other's house and I'd noticed that it was comfortable for us both. We hadn't spoken of our relationship any further as far as the context. Samantha said, 'I love you.' I didn't. I just hadn't found the appropriate time to say it. I thought that I was in love with her, but I wanted to be sure. So, I just kept my mouth shut. I would tell her when the time was right.

The phone rang. It was Sam.

"Want to meet me for lunch? I want to make love to you passionately on my desk" She asked cheerily.

"Sure, Babe, that would be great."

"I won't be free until two though, I have a late appointment and won't be done till about then. Meet me at the house?"

"Sure, I'll see you there." I said and we hung up.

I knew there would be no eating on this lunch, so I went into the other room and asked, "You up for ordering in?"

"Well, what are ya having?" she said.

Oh great...here we went. Every day lunch was an ordeal if I ate in. Monica was the worst decision maker on a simple level that I had ever met, besides me. Eating was something you had to do when Samantha wasn't around and I just ate. There was no real excitement to it.

"I'm having a veggie sandwich and potato salad," I chimed in, knowing that she would say exactly what she did.

"OK, sounds good to me, make it two."

I could have said I was having shit on a shingle and she would have replied the same. She was cute, not even five foot tall and had hair longer than anyone I had ever seen. She was a shrewd businesswoman. Her office worked with sheer determination, organization and motivation. As far as the shelter work went, we were planning a huge Christmas fund-raiser and I had nearly a quarter of the funds generated for the shelter already. I had approximately three months to gain the rest so that the budget for the next year would be sufficient. I kept plugging away at my baby's dream, which was now becoming my own.

I called in the sandwiches as Monica meandered into my office. You could call it nothing but "meandered". She sort of swayed in and leaned against my doorway.

After I hung up the phone, she said, "Why are you eating lunch here today? Didn't you just get a phone call from Samantha? I know she told me this morning when she called that you would be meeting her this afternoon for a late lunch." she giggled.

"Well, we are, but we never really eat, we talk more than anything," I could not contain my smile.

"Oh, yea..." she shook her head, "I bet you do. Let's see, you average three lunches a week with her and you are gone for two to three hours...and eating is not a priority. I see," she hummed.

I just smiled shyly at her. I had become accustomed to her teasing.

"You two are quite charming together. Even Jeff thinks so."

We had been to her home a couple of times for dinner. Her husband, Jeff, was wonderful...and ten times worse than she was as far as teasing. They welcomed our "couple" status and it was nice to have that.

She said, "I have an idea, Darlin. Why don't you and I give Sam a big surprise?" I could see her eyes glimmer with sheer evil as she grinned.

"What do you have in mind?"

I knew it would be better than anything I could think up. She laid out the plan and we put them in force as the sandwiches showed up. We ate together and talked about how much fun this would be and how much we loved seeing Samantha smile.

"Monica, I can't believe you can come up with something like this. Do you and Jeff do things like this?"

"OH, please. I tried to be romantic with Jeff in the beginning and just plain realized that nothing on this good earth would make that man appreciate anything other than his beer and football. So, I let him have them and do this kind of stuff to get my giggles." She packed up her sandwich stuff and tossed it in the wastebasket. "You just have fun and I will meet Jeff when he gets home naked. That usually lets him know I am in the mood."

I finished work and headed out at one o'clock. I had an hour to put this plan into action, Monica doing her part from the office. Every time Sam calls for a two o'clock lunch, I know she's already eaten and she's done for the day. So, our little afternoon would be fun. It was good stress relief/

I got my part set up. I knew Monica would set hers up also...you could count on that.

She walked in the door at two o'clock on the nose. She walked in and laid her things down on the antique chair, I knew her routine now. I was in the kitchen when she came in.

"I'm in here honey." I said.

"Hi, Baby," she walked up to me and kissed my cheek and patted my behind. "What're you doing? You look busy."

She was getting bottled water out of the fridge, peeking up over the door. I was washing fruit off and putting it in a big bowl. We had grapes, peeled oranges, apple slices and strawberries. I finished rinsing the fruit and dried my hands.

"I missed you, Samantha." I kissed her passionately and held her close. The days were good, coming home to her.

She slammed me up against the cabinet, catching me off balance. "I missed you too, my love." She was removing pieces of my clothing as we kissed. There were pieces of clothes dropping on the floor. She had me almost half undressed, before I remembered the plan.

"Oh, Honey, stop...please, " I muttered, squelched by her lips against mine. I found her hand and pulled her with me, taking the bowl of fruit in the other hand.

We moved toward the back of the house, Samantha badgering me the whole way. She snapped my bra strap, she pinched my butt; she grabbed the back of my pants, a pair of cream slacks, and yanked me back to her to kiss me. She had me pushed up against the hall wall and pressed my breasts hard with her hands, pushing me more into the wall. All I wanted to do was give her the afternoon I had planned and here she was less than cooperative.

"Abby, I want you so bad," she whispered hoarsely into my ear.

I moaned softly. Every time she touched me I felt the same, I needed her to touch me. When she wasn't around, I found myself feeling her touch or thinking about making love to her.

"I have a surprise for you." I said. She didn't let up.

She was intent upon making love right there in the hallway. It was as if something was wrong. She wasn't feeling my reactions. I could tell a difference in her usual demeanor. I stopped kissing her and took her face in my hands.

We sort of slid to the floor. I was trying to catch her eyes, but she was kissing my hands as I held her face. I kept trying to tip her face towards mine, but she was reluctant, her hands roving over my stomach.

"Samantha," I said softly but curtly. "What's wrong? Baby, talk to me, what's wrong?"

She was moving her face down again as I tried to lift it.

"Are you okay?" I was beginning to worry. Something was wrong. I waited patiently for her to look at me, loosening my grip to my hands lying against her face. Stroking her soft cheek. I felt a tear. "Samantha, please talk to me. Are you okay? Is something wrong?"

She made no move to answer, but lifted her face to mine and I saw intense pain.

"Jesus baby, what's wrong?" I had to know now. Something had happened, it was clear that something was wrong. I stayed where I was in case she was upset with me in some manner until she moved toward me assuring me it wasn't to do with me. She put her arms around me and sobbed.

I had cried more in the last month than in the last seventeen years. We were so emotional together.

"I missed you today, Abby," she was choking on her words as she wept out loud.

It was scaring me. Why was she hurting so badly?

"I love you, please don't leave me. I couldn't bare you leaving me Abby, promise me you won't...promise me," she whispered.

I didn't know what to say. I wasn't going anywhere and I hadn't said anything. What was the problem here? I took her hand and led her to the bathroom. I sat her down on the step to the bathtub, where I had run us a bath and had candles lit and music playing softly. I got a cold rag and wiped her eyes as I knelt in front of her. I kissed her softly on the cheek.

"Sam, did something happen today?" I asked.

She nodded her head, "No, nothing." she hiccupped out. "I was in my office today and I was sitting there smiling. Tommy came in and was sitting there with me. He was talking about nothing; he comes in sometimes and just sits while I do paperwork. I was sitting there, Abby, talking to him..." Her eyes registered an even deeper pain. "I want a family..." She sobbed again.

She threw her arms around me and sobbed uncontrollably. "I want a baby and I want a family and I want it all with you." She was hysterical.

She seemed like someone I barely knew.

"Samantha, Darling, look at me..." I trailed my words as I lifted her chin, tipped it, so she could see me. "Baby, I ran a bath for us, let's slide in and I'll just hold you. Come with me and relax. Let's talk, okay?" I said.

I urged her with my hands in hers to climb to her feet. She was still crying softly, but she got up. I undressed her slowly, kissing her softly as I removed the rest of her clothing. I liked taking off her work clothes. It was like taking the work face off her for the most part. She always looked so classy, never disheveled. We could make love for hours and she would still come up looking like she was fresh. Me, however, my hair would be mussed against my head, my face would be flushed, and my eyes would barely open, as if I was drunk. She didn't have that problem and she would tease me profusely. She always kept her demeanor.

She started to follow suit with me and began to undress me the rest of the way. She looked at me, gazed into my eyes, as she unbuttoned my slacks...the zipper's quiet purr was all I heard before they fell off my hips and her hands caressed them. Her eyes never left mine as she unfastened my bra and slid it off my shoulders. She didn't say a word.

She then moved to her panties, which were all that was left on her and slid her index finger under the waistband, I caught it in my peripheral vision as I looked deeply in her eyes, the fear now gone. She traced the line of her panties with her finger before she removed them and moved to mine, sliding them gracefully off my hips and slowly down my thighs. She let them drop and I stepped out of them. She did the same. In our nakedness we embraced.

I took her hand and we walked the steps as the music drifted lightly in the room. The candles burned as our light. I washed her eyes, my concern more for her. We slid into the bath, sitting face to face as we washed each other. She gently moved the soap over my body, slowly and deliberately. She watched my eyes and felt my reaction.

This time as she had in the past, not aggressively trying to forget as in the hallway. There was no sexual connotation to the washing. I washed her in the same manner, paying close attention to her shoulders and breast, removing her tension.

She closed her eyes as I washed. I was realizing how much I loved this woman. I had not said the words yet. I wanted to, but I was afraid. I was so afraid of what she meant to me and losing her. I had lost so much in my life. I knew it was time to let all of that go. I would tell her I loved her soon. She had fears too, I knew now. But, I didn't know what they were. It was time to find out. She was my priority, not me or my past.

I prompted her to speak to me by my gentle words, "Samantha, I care about you so much. Do you know that?"

Her gaze began to explore my eyes, to look deep in my soul. "Abby, I want that so much, but I have such insecurity about it." She was not a woman of fear. "I'm afraid Abby. I'm terrified that I'll never have what I want in this life. It's been so lonely."

Her eyes misted, but the tears did not fall. "I've had love, but never love that lasted. My father wasn't capable and he killed my mother. My grandmother was wonderful to me, but it was a job to her. She took me, because she had to. Not because she wanted to."

She still held eye contact. I said nothing, and did not break the contact, it wasn't threatening at all.

"Lauren wasn't loving. She was secure. I had no idea that loving someone was like this, Abby. I miss you when you aren't with me. I want healthy, but I find my thoughts drifting to you each and every moment we aren't together. You haven't left my home or me yours, except to work since the fifteenth. It's been almost a month. I still have a burning for you that won't go away," she spoke even softer, almost to an inaudible state "I don't want it to." She stared at me, looking for an answer.

"I won't leave you Samantha. Is that what you are afraid of?" I asked.

I was as soft as I could be, reaching for her hands under the water. The water was warm, the music was soft and the candles were gentle in our moment.

"I promise you, I won't leave you. I wanted my whole life to find someone like you, not someone I could live with, but someone I couldn't live without. Do not be afraid," I said as the front doorbell rang.

I had forgotten about Monica's part of the plan. "Shit! Give me a few minutes, Sweetie."

I ran from the tub, grabbed a towel, and ran to the front

door, dripping wet. I left Sammie sitting in the bath without so much as an explanation.

I opened the door just a tad and thanked the man for coming and told him we would be out in just a moment. I started back for the bathroom, but Samantha met me in the hall with a wondering gaze. I laughed.

"Sorry, honey, I forgot about the rest of the plans." I said.

We had spent more time than I had even imagined. It was five-thirty now. The fruit had gone to waste again.

"What are we doing?" Her gaze was intent and playful again.

We hadn't finished discussing and yet she seemed more assured. I had wanted to tell her that I loved her. And, once again, it was the heat of the moment, and the moment had passed

"Where are we going? What have you done now?" She said.

She was toying with me again. She loved my surprises. I had left notes on the mirror in the mornings, or in the fridge for her to find. She had done similar things; it was so wonderful having someone return the favors of love. I had been quite content, but still not sure that this would last forever. In the past, I had thought it would be and it hadn't.

"Well, I planned an afternoon in the bath and some fruit. I was going to show you how to eat fruit the right way." I whined.

She had a look of devilishness about her, "Are you suggesting I do not know my fruit? I might add, I think I know how to eat it. As a matter of fact, let me see..." Her words followed her back into the bathroom.

I had already finished putting on my bra and panties and had a pair of jeans ready to slide into, when she came running from the bathroom and tackled me to the bed. She was laughing again.

I played as if I were annoyed by her attention, "Samantha!!! We've had plans all day and you have now thwarted them all. What ARE you trying to do?"

She was unaffected by my attitude. She pushed me down to the bed and held my upper arms. I could see that she had a few grapes in her mouth.

She held my legs with hers, stronger than I had remembered for some reason and my arms with hers as she let her hair fall on my stomach. It was wet and cold, the touch of her hair sending chills over my entire body. She was teasing me, slowly. She loved to tease me and she knew it worked. I was so impatient; I wanted her to touch me. I couldn't really move though, the weight of her body on mine. She was running her tongue all over me, but never touched my breasts, still held by my navy lace bra. I could see the grapes in her cheeks...and then she looked at me. She dropped a grape between her teeth. She was wicked and her eyes reflected that. She moved her head, ever so slowly, to my chest, between my breasts and let the grape drip as she bit into it gently. She watched me as I watched her. The juice dripped down warm from being in her mouth. Then she ate the grape. Chewing so I could watch, acting as if it were the most luscious thing she'd ever had touch her tongue. When she finished, she took another grape, dropping it between her teeth from her cheek, the last grape. She let it drop between my breasts. She moved to kiss me lightly, teasing. I wanted more... but she refused. She then moved back to the grape. She rolled the grape with her tongue to the left just at the edge of my bra. I watched intently. She tucked the grape up under my bra, slid it in-between my skin and the material and moved it with her teeth so gently to where it sat just above my nipple.

She then came back and kissed me again, leaning slowly towards my lips, her eyes closed. Never quite touching my lips with hers as I leaned forward.

"I thought you might like a little sample of my grape eating capabilities, Sugar." She said and was gone again, headed back to the grape. As she sat, poised over the grape, holding my gaze again, she licked her lips.

"Are you ready, Abby?" She asked me.

Oh yes, I was ready in every way. I had forgotten about the carriage and the carriage driver outside waiting to take us to dinner.

"Yes." I muttered softly.

She bit down on the grape and let the juice run over me. She then sucked all the juice off, over my bra. It was the most arousing sensation. And then she got up, let go of me and started to dress. She left me lying on the bed!

She was half dressed, wearing a pair of old Levi jeans, faded and worn.

"You might want to dress warm, Sweetie. Your evil and wicked...leaving me on that bed alone...I said as I scampered up from the bed.

She looked at me now, questioning me.

"Sam, did you forget about someone knocking on the door, while we were in the bath?" I asked.

She smiled. "I thought you took care of them. Who was it?"

I laughed and told her to dress quickly as I dressed too. We put on jeans and sweaters and boots. Her sweater was cream and green and mine was gray wool. Both were big and baggy. I had been surprised in the last month with the comfort that she dressed at home, especially when she got so dressed up for work. She didn't look the part right now. The sweater set her eyes off tremendously. She didn't put any accessories on other than what she had on already: the necklace I had given her, gold hoop earrings, and a gold bracelet. We grabbed our coats as we headed out the door.

She was locking up when she turned around to see the horse drawn carriage parked in front of the house on the street. It was nearly six o'clock and I knew Monica had made reservations at the restaurant at seven. How did the plan get so messed up? She grabbed my coat as we came to the screened porch door.

"Abby, you love me, don't you?" she looked at me with the same look that had taken her to tears before.

I shook my head, because I did. I started to say it again, I started to say the words, but she kissed me. She kissed me gently and held me for a brief moment.

"Thank you, Abby. I thought you did." And we left.

The carriage ride was wonderful. The driver took us directly to the restaurant, which took nearly forty minutes. We had originally been planning that the ride would last longer and we would tour the park, but time restraints prevented it. I told Sam of the original plan.

She pouted again. This woman pouted like no one I had ever met. Her bottom lip came flying out and her lashes grew at least and inch as she batted them at me. They were dark with mascara and really stood out. Her lip was so kissable. I reached over and bit it playfully. The driver didn't seem to notice.

We held hands and said very little. It was a comfortable silence. At dinner, we had the same. A little out of the way restaurant that only seated about twenty in its capacity. We noticed nothing. We were driven to distraction with each other. We sat at a small corner booth, on the same side of the table, held hands and sipped our wine and then ate. It was so romantic.

The candlelight, the soft jazz playing throughout the restaurant created an exquisite ambiance. We talked of how our work was going and how much we enjoyed each other's company.

She whispered, "I love you so much, Abby." as the waiter pulled up the dessert cart.

I was starting to get annoyed with the distractions that came when I wanted to tell her I loved her. The moment had to be right. And now here he was.

We declined dessert, paid our bill and ventured back out into the night. I had sent the driver away with a very nice tip prior to entering the restaurant, so we walked home. We walked through the park, hand-in-hand. She sang to me; a song I didn't know, but it was familiar. It was mostly humming, but the words said:

Gently I whisper from across the water,
Waiting for a reply of effort on your part.
I cannot come to you...love waiting for a start...

And then she hummed. It was beautiful. The hair on the back of my neck stood up.

"Abby, do you think about the future?" she looked at me as we walked.

"Yes, I do. And you are part of my future Samantha. I know that." I said.

She squeezed my hand as we walked. She babbled the rest of the way home about the shelter and how wonderful it was to plan the new and exciting things. She talked of how she was going to do things and where she was putting her dreams. I was falling deeper and deeper.

Chapter Fourteen

"Abby, are you there? Pick up the phone. Shit, please pick up the phone..." Desiree's voice chimed on the answering machine.

I grabbed for the phone as Samantha grabbed the alarm clock to get a better look at what time it was.

"Hello, Des, what's wrong?" I said.

Sam showed me it was four-fifteen in the morning. We had been in deep sleep mode and were still groggy.

"She left me, Abby..." She started crying. "She left me..." Des sounded exhausted and partially drunk.

"Where are you, Des?" I asked.

"Is she okay?" Sammie whispered.

I shook my head no. She wasn't okay, I could tell that in her voice.

"Des, where are you? I'm coming to get you." A bolt of fear jetted through my body. The last time this happened, I had to pick her bleeding body up off the floor and hold her until the ambulance came, she had tried to kill herself. It was four years ago and it numbed me to hear her in this type of situation. Fear was motivational.

"Desiree, don't piss me off. Where are you?" I was stern.

"I'm at home." She slurred. "You don't need to come get me. I won't do it again. The bitch had an affair on me and left me for that fucking art bitch." She wailed.

"Well, can I come get you? Sam will make some coffee and I'll pick you up and bring you here. Why don't you stay with us for the weekend?" I said.

It was Friday night and there was nothing worse that a lonely weekend breakup with nothing to take your mind off it.

"Okay..." She said in the same slur. "I can't do this again, Abby. I just can't take it. My family found out about everything and cut me off once. I can't take more scandal. Even when it isn't something that is publicized, I still look the fool." She started sobbing.

"Talk to Sammie until I get there, Sweetie. Give me five minutes. I'm on my way." I handed Samantha the phone and heard her kick into crisis mode.

She was used to this and she could keep her attention until I was there. Something was wrong. Desiree sounded different. The first thing that ran through my mind was sleeping pills.

I wrote a quick note on the pad beside the bed: *If she passes out, hang up and call 911...I have a bad feeling on this one. Don't hesitate.*

She mouthed, "I won't. I love you."

I zipped out the door, only grabbing my purse, coat and keys. Dressed in boxers and a t-shirt, I was in my car in seconds and it was freezing. I started it and moved fast. I had an urgent need for speed. Des lived over by the cabin. It would take me at least twenty minutes to get there.

"Shit. Shit. Shit!!! Don't do this to me, Desiree. Damn it." I pounded my fists on my steering wheel. "I can't handle this again, Des. Don't make me think about it again..."

I had, at one time, found myself deciding that anytime my life went good, someone had to die. I had just moved past that a couple of years ago, but my life had been so miserable. Now that I was happy, it couldn't happen again. Nine deaths in eight years were too many. "NOT AGAIN..." I screamed, as I turned up the music as loud as I could get it and flew through stoplights and drove down the street at over 90 mph. I had a feeling on this one.

How I saw it, I didn't know, but out of the corner of my eye, I caught the light on my cell phone, which was charging in the seat next to me, flash with a call coming in.

"Hello." I turned the music down to answer.

"Baby, it's me...head to St. Paul's Hospital. She passed out. She took some sleeping pills; I got that much out of her. I used the cell and called on her right after you left. I could tell by your face that it was out of control and didn't want to take a chance. I talked to them while they talked to her, but she passed out."

"Okay."

"I'm going to meet you there; I love you, Baby. I will be right there." She said, without giving me a chance to say anything. She was beginning to know me well. In the two months we had known each other, we had talked and communicated more than in any relationship that I had ever had.

"Sam, not now, not before the holidays. I hate the holidays. What am I going to do?" I started crying.

I hit the steering wheel again. I got so angry.

"Abby, she is with the best help she can get. I think it will be fine. They are taking her in, because they can't tell how much alcohol she had on top of it." Sam said.

"Okay. Okay..." I said.

"I'm on my cell right now and about half way there, Honey. Where are you at?" She asked me.

I had turned around and wasn't more than a couple of minutes away.

"I'm almost there. How far out are you?" I asked.

"I am five blocks away at the most. Be careful, Abby." She said.

"Just talk to me, Sam. Talk me there." I was afraid.

"I am right here, Abby. I am going to be there before you; meet me at the ER driveway. I'm going to pull up where I park when they bring a crisis call in. I can see it from here." She said.

I heard her tires screech, she must have pulled into the parking lot. I was about a block away. I punched the accelerator and the Mazda flew the next block with ease. I saw the Rodeo as I whipped into the parking lot. She was standing beside the truck waiting for me.

"I see you." I said.

"Hang up and park, Babe." She said and hung up.

I did and pulled into the space next to her; she was moving towards the electric doors as I got out and I followed.

"She should be in ER. I'm going to ask at the desk and see if we can get in. Say you are her sister." She said as she ran next to me.

I was clad in only my boxers, tee and coat. I had on tennis shoes and realized for the first time that I had nothing on underneath. I was feeling very vulnerable, like I could burst into tears at any moment.

"Hurry, Samantha."

"Do you have a Desiree Carlton-Webber that just came in?" She asked the woman behind the desk.

The woman ignored her while she continued working on some paperwork.

"I don't believe you heard me, Miss. Do you have a Desiree Carlton-Webber, who just came in? I am with the Crisis Center and I need to get her sister into see her." Sam motioned to me.

"She just came in, they have her in room three." She pointed around the corner.

"Thank you." She said as she grabbed my hand and we moved quickly down the corridor to room three.

As we burst into the room, we saw them trying to shove a tube down her nose. Des was down on the table and unconscious.

"Is she okay?" I blurted.

The nurse grabbed us and escorted us to the door. "They are pumping her stomach. After that we'll know more. We drew blood to see what's in her system and we will determine what we can in the immediate future. She has an IV and so far that is all we've done." She said.

She was trying to push us from the room as we heard Des screaming...in pain.

"Stop." Des was pushing at the nurse trying to administer the tube.

She began to cry.

"We need to know what you took. Can you tell us what you ingested?" The nurse said pulling the tube out as carefully as possible.

"If you cooperate with us, we will determine what to do from there." Another nurse interjected.

"I...What? Where am I?" Des was coming to. She saw us standing there. "Abby help me. Tell them I'm okay." She said.

I moved closer to her. "What did you take, Honey? Tell them what you took." I pleaded.

"I didn't take anything. I had two sleeping pills and a couple of drinks; I don't know." She said.

The nurse scooted us out into the hallway. "You might want to wait in the waiting room and we will come and get you when we know something. Since she's conscious that's a pretty good sign. I'll come out and get you as soon as we know anything." She said.

We moved into the waiting room. I laid my head on Samantha when she put her arm around me after sitting next to me in a chair.

"She scared me, Sam." I started to mist up.

"She's going to be okay, Darling. With her being awake now, she will be okay. I know she scared you. You have dealt with a lot of loss. It's okay." She kissed my head.

She started to laugh a bit.

"What?" I said.

"Look at how we're dressed." She pointed to my legs.

I had nothing but the boxers and T-shirt on and my lightweight coat. It was freezing cold outside and I was clad in barely anything. I looked at Samantha. When we went to bed last night, we had made love and I had taken her shirt off. I didn't remember her putting it back on.

"Do you have a shirt on?" I asked.

She smiled and opened her coat a bit to reveal nothing but skin. She had on a pair of shorts, but nothing else. I laughed with her a little.

"I tried to grab the cell phone and my purse and I saw my coat laying on the floor where I dropped it last night when we got home. You attacked me at the door and I didn't think about anything else, but catching you before you got to Des' house." She said.

"At least you got here fast. I would have freaked out if I had had to come here with her again. It was too close last time. She had called me and she passed out while we were on the phone and then I went to her house, not really knowing what I would find. I found her on the floor in a mess; she had thrown up all over herself. She took a bunch of pills and I didn't know what to do. I thought she was dying in my arms and I finally remembered 911 and waited for them to get there. She had tried to cut her wrists, but was probably too drunk and messed up. The blood scared me more than anything. They wouldn't let me in with her, because I wasn't related." I said. "I waited for two days, she wouldn't wake up. Finally they got her stabilized and let me in with her. Jenny did the same thing. I know this is stupid, but I can't stand it when this kind of thing happens. It scares me more than I care to think possible." I noticed my hands were shaking and I could feel the tremors from the inside of my body moving out. I hated that feeling, shaking from the inside out. My teeth were chattering, but not from the cold.

"Honey, I am here now, and it's okay." Sam said and stroked my hair.

We waited for almost two hours and then a nurse finally came in and got us so we could talk to Des. It was almost seven in the morning.

Des spoke to us immediately upon our entering the room, "Where have you been?"

"Are you okay?" I asked.

"Yeah. I don't know what happened. I was so tired and I hadn't been able to sleep, so I took a couple of pills. I guess I had drunk too much before. I called you and things just got fuzzy. The next thing I know someone is shoving a tube down my throat and then they take you away. Lord, it has been a mess convincing them that I didn't try and kill myself again." She said. She looked exhausted.

"I get to go home in about ten minutes. They went to get some aftercare papers and then I'm free to go." She said.

"You are going home with us. We are both off work tomorrow, the whole weekend, actually, and you are coming home with us and getting some sleep. I won't take no for an answer, Desiree." Samantha said.

"I won't fight you. I don't wanna be alone." She said with a weak smile. "I don't know why she did it. I thought she meant it last time when she said it would never happen again, Abby. I trusted her."

"I know, Des." I said. "We will figure it out. Do you want us to wait in here or outside?" I asked.

"You can wait out in the waiting room. I shouldn't be but a few more minutes and it's really cold in here." She tried to smile.

"Here, take my coat." I gave her my coat. "It isn't like you can take Samantha's." Sam and I laughed and Sam flashed her really fast.

Des's face lit up and she burst into a little giggle. "Holy shit. Now that made it all worth it. Get out of here." She motioned towards the door, still smiling.

❦

We sat at the kitchen table, after Sam and I slept in shifts, all three of us in the same bed. Desiree was out like a light once we got her back to the house and Samantha held me while I cried.

"Well, so what do we do?" Samantha said, sipping her coffee.

I shrugged my shoulders. "What happened exactly, Des? How did you find out?"

Des took a big gulp of hot coffee, "Well, she called last night and told me that she wouldn't be coming home last night...or ever again. She said I could throw away her things or give them to Salvation Army? She didn't care; she's not coming home. We had gotten into a big fight about how she was not communicating with me lately. She closed herself off. For the last two weeks, she'd been sleeping on the couch. I couldn't figure out what happened. It was like she just quit the relationship again." She said.

"How did Tabrai come into all this?" Sam said.

"Well, I asked where she was going to go, if she wasn't coming home and she said that she would be staying with her." Des hissed out the word 'her'.

"So, do you know that they are together, or is she just staying with her?" I asked.

She shrugged. "I don't know. Jenny said that she wasn't with her, but I know how fast it happened last time and I don't trust it. It's the same thing as before. Except before, she took all her things while I was away for the weekend and I came home to a note. At least I didn't get a note this time." She said.

The phone rang.

"Excuse me." Sam moved to get the phone in the living room.

"You know, there could be worse things. I know that you don't want to hear that, but there are many things that are worse than losing a relationship. I don't want you to be sad, but I want you to be in the present too. This is hard, but things usually have a way of working out." I tried to encourage her.

"I know. And, we really have been having problems the last six months. She wants to find herself. She thinks that her 'creative energy is being stifled, because of my political aspirations'. What she really means, is that now that I am campaigning, I am never home. And it's true. This part of the career is hard to take. But we all know it has its perks." Des said.

Sam stood at the doorway. "Honey, can you come here for a moment? You're wanted on the phone."

I moved to the living room, but as I passed Sam she said, "It's Jenny. I didn't know what to tell her."

"Oh shit." I whispered.

I moved into the living room and took the phone. "Jenny, hi." I said.

"What's going on, Abby? I heard she was taken by ambulance last night. I went over to pick up some things and Jasper, the neighbor to the right asked me how she was. I freaked out. What happened? I called the hospital and they told me she had been admitted and released." Jenny said.

"Well, it was a false alarm. Nothing happened. She just wasn't feeling well." I said.

"Did she try and kill herself again? I know what happened last time, she told me." Jenny said.

"No. I thought she did, but jumped the gun on her and really made a mess of things. She just passed out from drinking too much. It really was no big deal." I said. "But, I do have a question for you, Jenny. You know that I love Des with all my heart...what the hell's going on?" I said.

"Nothing, Abby. I can't do this anymore. She doesn't want a girlfriend, she wants someone to hang on her arm and that isn't me. I want to be my own person. I'm not with Tabrai and she keeps saying that I am. I just came here to stay instead of fight with her." She started crying. "I thought I lost her this morning when they told me the ambulance came. I just want to know if she will see me so that we can talk. She jumps to such conclusions. I just want to talk to her. And, Samantha said she didn't know if it was a good idea. What do you think, Abby? Do we talk this out or do I just leave for good?"

I thought about it for a minute. I thought they loved each other and I wanted Des and Jenny both to be happy.

"Give me two minutes and then call back. I'm going to go talk to her and see what she wants to do. Okay?" I asked.

"Sure. I can do that." She said and hung up.

I went back into the kitchen and Des was crying in Samantha's arms. Sam looked at me with pitiful eyes. She was patting Des' back. "There, there Des. It's okay. Just talk to her, Honey. Tell her how you feel." She said.

To see one of the political realms best representatives brought to tears over a woman was amazing. Des was so astute in her career. And, here she was crying over someone cheating, who apparently wasn't cheating. Smart girls made such stupid lovers.

"That was Jenny on the phone, Des." I said.

Des brought her head up quickly to look at me. "What does *she* want?" She hissed.

"Des. In my opinion, I think you need to talk to her. She

says she isn't with Tabrai and you need to at least listen to her. I know that you two love each other and that is all that counts. Please talk to her." I suggested.

"I don't want to talk to her. I don't understand anything she says and I don't want to be anymore confused than I am now. I know she was with Tabrai. There isn't a question in my mind. Why else would she have stayed there with her?" She said.

"Well, did you ever think of asking her? Are you going to throw away all the time you have with her on something that you are assuming?" Samantha said.

"I agree with Samantha. Aren't you at least gonna let her explain? She thought you checked out last night and when she found out that you were okay, maybe that made her realize her error and let her have time to think things through. Listen to her. What will it hurt?" I said.

"How am I supposed to talk to her? Will you two be there with us, so that we can at least stay calm? We just yell and get nowhere. Will you help us?" She asked.

"I don't' know." I said looking at Samantha for an answer.

"You can have your meeting here, but we will refrain from being present unless we hear raised voices. You two are adults and can act as such. You can mediate here, but I think it's something you should do on your own. How else will you be able to communicate with each other later? I think it might just be a crutch. We can always come in and suggest calmness if things get out of hand. I think I am more comfortable with that." Sam said.

"That sounds better to me." I said as the phone rang again.

This time, I picked it up in the kitchen.

"Hello." I said. "Hold on a second, Jenny. Let me get her." I handed the phone to Des.

"Hello..." She said in a small voice. "Uh huh...Okay. Four o'clock here is fine." She said.

She handed me back the phone. I placed it on its cradle.

❧

"I just want to sit on the porch all day long like this. Let's quit our jobs and just become part of the porch. Do you think anyone would notice? We could just watch the people walk and drive by. No one would notice us, we would just be part of the lawn furniture." Sam said.

"I think that would be nice." I said as I lay back in the chair soaking up the winter sun. It was cold but not so cold you couldn't sit comfortably in the sun. We decided to soak up some rays while the girls talked. Desiree was in taking a shower and we came out to the porch, still in our pajamas.

"Nothing like Boxer-bathing. Huh?" I said.

She laughed lightly. "I can think of a better bathing, but we have to wait until Des gets out of the shower. You game?" She asked.

I knew exactly what she meant. Showering together with her was dangerous. It always started out as just a calm shower and then ended up with us on the floor in the bathroom soaking wet, making love. It was not something I was immune to yet. She was too tempting naked. I couldn't keep myself away from her. We still made love every chance we got. I never would tire of her; that I was sure of.

"I think you are being wicked again. And, I know I don't want to tarnish my halo anymore than it already is. I'm such an angel." I joked.

"Oh, please. Angel my butt, I know how much tarnish that halo has on it. Most days I can't walk you are such an angel." She said as she sat soaking up the sun with her sunglasses hiding her eyes.

"If Jenny wasn't going to pull up any second, I would come over there and show you how much of an angel I am." I teased her.

"You better stay over there on your side of this table, in your own chair, or I am going to make you sorry you didn't." She said. "Last night was completely unfair. No one makes me orgasm seven times in a row and then won't let me touch them. I can't believe you did that to me." She 'hummphed' me and then continued. "I couldn't believe how much it did to me watching you touch yourself. I think eight, nine and ten were without being touched." She laughed.

"You know, I am sitting here thinking...What if the girls at the shelter knew you were this way? I bet they would pay big for information like this." I teased again.

"You think they don't know? Miranda makes me give her details each day. She thinks you are some sort of super-human-lesbian. She thinks that I am insatiable." She laughed.

"What?" I was shocked. "You talk about us to them?"

She was laughing again, "I was just teasing you. I can't tell them that we make love at night rather than have dinner, that we shower together and never come out without making love or that there hasn't been a day that at work I haven't thought about making love to you on the desk. Even when I used to think of you before I called you that night, I used to fantasize about you and me and that desk. Too bad I love my job so much. I have had you so many times on that desk that I am surprised it's still standing."

"Oh my God, you are such a nymph." I was laughing with her. "I can't believe you fantasized about me. You probably did it all those nights that you called me into the shelter to work when there was a full staff?" I said.

"You got that right. You still don't know everything about my calling you in those nights. I would sit there and debate about even calling you. Finally I would get up the nerve to call you and then I would sit there and plan out how I would ask you to dinner. In my mind, I played that out so many times and when I actually did it I had it played out so perfectly. I chickened out on it; every plan I had I chickened out, with the exception of feeding you. But after I kissed you, I couldn't think of anything but making love to you and I wanted so badly to be the good girl and not scare you away. You looked so afraid the first time I came up to you and kissed you." She was laughing more this time. "You should have seen your face. You were sweating bullets. I thought you were going to bolt on me, right out the door. And, then when I ran the bath for you. I was going to strip for you and climb in with you when I brought the 'orgasms' in.

But, you looked like a frightened bird trying to get all down in the bubbles; I couldn't do it. So, I left you alone. I had never had to make the first move before and I was incredibly chicken. After you came out of the bath and had on my clothes and looked so cute, I couldn't resist. And, I am glad that I didn't. I think I love you more, because you were frightened than if it had been a piece of cake. You definitely kept me on my toes."

Before I could answer to that, Jenny's car blew into the drive, bouncing over the curb and nearly taking out the mailbox.

"What in the world?" Samantha said. "That girl is crazy."

Sam had only met Jenny the one time. It seemed that Jenny's wild side hadn't really shown its face. I knew Jenny to be young and carefree. Her old beat up car, her pride and joy, probably wasn't more than three years old. It was beat up, because she couldn't drive. Des used to make so many jokes about how bad Jenny drove, until it would piss Jenny off enough for them to fight. Des finally learned her lesson and it wasn't spoken of. Jenny just wasn't 'allowed' to drive the new vehicles.

Jenny bounded up the drive with Tabrai.

"Uh oh..." Samantha said.

"This kid isn't big on brains, is she?" I said in reply.

We got up and greeted them.

"Hi, Abby...you remember Tabrai. Samantha, good to see you." She hugged us each. Tabrai stood shyly at the door of the porch.

"Come on in." I motioned to Tabrai and offered her my lawn chair. "Jenny, let me show you in." I escorted Jenny into the house and left Sammie and Tabrai on the porch.

Once inside, I found Des sitting at the kitchen table, no makeup and wet hair and looking like she had been through quite an ordeal. My best guess was that she cried herself through the shower.

"Here you go, Jenny." I offered her a chair at the table. "Can I get you some coffee or juice, water or anything?" I said.

"Juice would be fine. Thank you." She said to me and turned to Des. "Des, I'm sorry." She started in.

I tried to block the conversation as much as possible. I got the juice, handed it to her and said, "We will be right outside. No fighting, got it? You two are here to talk this out. Listen to each other and make the most of this, I know you love each other and this is the time to prove it. Listen to each other."

Back out on the porch, Samantha and Tabrai were talking about meeting that night at the gallery. I didn't rush out onto the porch, but eavesdropped on part of the conversation.

I heard Sam saying, "Looking at you sort of freaks me out. I was born in Russia and it was eerie looking at you. I felt like I was looking in the mirror ten years ago." She stopped.

"Yes, I know what you say." Tabrai's accent was very thick. "I do not realize it until one of the gentleman from the gallery ask me if you my sister. I then took a good look at you and came to introduce myself. I look like you." She said.

I moved out onto the porch. I wondered to myself if Samantha had thought about the fact that both of them were actually from Russia? Wouldn't it be weird if they were somehow related?

"Honey, we were just chatting. Come sit with me." Samantha patted her chair and slid her legs over the side so that I could sit between them.

We then spoke of Jenny and Des and each gave our take on the situation, all relatively close to the same decision, that Jenny just needed some space and Des worked too much.

The ladies all left about an hour later and the conclusion that Jenny and Des had drawn was that they needed to separate for a month and see what happened at the end of that time. Des had agreed to go to counseling with Jenny and they were going to work on things.

❧

Monday morning I was in my office working and the phone rang.

"Hello, this is Abby, can I help you please?" I answered, my mind still on the paperwork in front of me.

"Honey, do you have a few moments?" Samantha purred into my phone.

"Well, of course I do, Sugar. What's up?" I said putting aside the papers.

"I'm going to go to North Carolina...today." She said.

A bolt of electricity shot through my body. What in the world? What did that mean? Going to North Carolina for what? Did I do something wrong?

She must have realized my reaction, she said, "I have to go on business. I wanted to call you; I want to see you before I leave. I just talked to my attorney and he wants to meet with me later tonight. He has some papers for me dealing with some family involvement." She stopped for a moment.

"Is everything okay, Sammie?" I asked.

"Oh, heavens yes, I just need to go take care of some paperwork, I should do this alone. I'm not trying to be secretive, but for some reason I just can't spit out what it's for. I was going to have him just deliver it here, but then I decided that I might need some help with it. Well, I don't know what to do? I'm so confused...do you want to go with me? I haven't made my reservations yet." She said.

"What's going on, Sammie. I would love to go with you, if you want me to?" I was completely confused. When I left for work today we talked about how much work both of us had to do before we left for the holidays in two weeks.

I said, "I can take my work with me. Did you free your schedule up?"

"Miranda is going to run things for a couple of days. Can you come over to the shelter and let me explain everything?" She said, a little frustrated.

"Are you sure you're okay, Samantha? You don't sound like yourself." I asked.

"Just come over and I'll tell you. It's a long story and I can't go into it on the phone." She said. "I don't know if I am okay or not. Just hurry over." She said.

"Okay, I'll be there as soon as I get this packed up and can drive over." I said and hung up.

I drove to the shelter, which is all of about ten minutes from the office and the whole time worried about what could have come up. Samantha didn't have any family to worry about, unless I didn't know about them, and there wasn't any unfinished business that I knew of that she had mentioned. I racked my brain; I wondered what might have come up.

Monica had agreed to take my calls and I would check messages and everything else was mobile. I had packed my case and my computer and my office became a moveable unit. I pulled up in front of the shelter feeling very uneasy about something.

I entered and asked Miranda where Sam was, she steered me to Sam's office.

"Hi..." I peeked around the corner, her door was open.

"Oh, Abby...I think I made a huge mistake. I can't do this." She said and moved behind me to shut the door and fell into my arms.

I held her; She had never displayed affection to me in her office or anywhere else in the shelter for that matter. I could feel her start to cry.

"What's wrong, Sammie?" I said.

She spoke, but I couldn't understand what she was saying, she was sobbing and trying to talk.

I moved her to the chair in front of her desk and pulled a Kleenex for her.

"Here, dry your eyes and tell me what's going on and then we will deal with it, Sam. Is it that bad?" I asked.

She used the Kleenex and handed it back to me, motioning for another. I obliged and she used the second and a third. She couldn't stop crying.

"On my desk," She hiccuped, "there is a fax. Read it." She said.

I looked on her desk, which was always organized and found a fax from her attorney in North Carolina. I read it quickly and found it to be a fulfillment to a request she had made about who her real mother was. He said that the information could be presented to her however she deemed it best.

I knelt down in front of her. She had her face in her hands, still crying softly.

"Sam, when did you request this?" I asked, stroking her hair, trying to be supportive.

She looked up at me, bright eyes filled with tears, spilling over and down her cheeks. "I don't know why I did it, now it's brought up too much for me, and I can't stop crying. I've been in here all day, a mess. Finally, I decided to just go home and face it all." She said.

"Do you think flooding like this is the way to do it? Can we talk about it, before you make any decisions? We could go for a walk?" I said, taking her hands in mine.

"A walk?" She said.

"Yeah, let's get you out of here and get some fresh air. There is the park just down the street. Let's walk down there and just sit and talk." I wanted her to trust me enough to talk about this. I knew how hard it was for me to bring up my past. Even though I had worked on it all, even though I had grieved a lot of it, I still didn't feel real comfortable talking about it.

"Okay." She said tears still sliding down her cheeks.

I kissed her forehead and helped her up and got her coat for her. I still had mine on. We left the shelter and walked the few blocks in silence. I wished I could hold her hand, but I couldn't. The residential area was too risky to display affection in.

I pushed her gently in the swing she had chosen, standing in front of her, shoving off her knees as she floated to me.

"I just thought that not knowing was worse than knowing and so I ordered the information. I knew my mother had kept everything and Dean had it all in his office. I called after we went to the gallery opening to see if he really did have the information telling me who my mother, well my birth mother, was?" She said.

"Why after the gallery showing, Sammie?" I asked.

"Because, Tabrai looked like me. Sometimes I meet people that resemble me and well, I could be related, you know?" Her eyes plead with me to understand as she swung softly on the swing. "I just want to know for sure. It's been a question I've had since my mother died, but I've been thinking about it a lot, because I want to have a baby. I just want to know." She said.

She had been talking about having a baby lately.

"What will you do once you know? Have you thought that far ahead?" I asked.

"Well, that is what hit me today. All of the sudden, it hit me, that I would know, and then what would I do? What if she died too? There are no guarantees. I could have this hope and find that she isn't even alive either. That would crush me. But, what if she is? I think I would benefit from knowing. I sat and talked to Tabrai yesterday and noticed my mannerisms and hers were so similar. I watched her talk with her hands and looked down at mine, they were the same hands. I mean our nails were shaped the same and the way our fingers were shaped, our body structure, all of it. We even have the same shape to our eyes. It really moved something in me." She said.

"Well, let's do it then. We can get through anything. I am here for you and we will deal with whatever we find out. We can look for your birthmother and see what we can find. The worst part of it would be not being able to find her. Right?" I said.

She shook her head. "Yes." She said.

"Have you thought about how hard it might be for you to actually find someone in Russia? There might be government interventions and things of that nature." I said.

"Well, I thought maybe Tabrai could help me. She's from Russia. Who knows, we might be related?" She laughed a little for the first time.

"That sounds like a good plan. Do you want my opinion?" I asked.

"Of course, Honey. I take great heed in what you think, feel and add to this relationship." She said, slowing the swing to a stop.

"I think that you should just get the information sent here, no need to travel and then I am here to deal with it with you and you're at home. You can take a couple of days to yourself and see what you can find out, maybe do some research and try and tie up what ends you can. You know this process could be long and tedious." I said.

"I understand. I don't know what the urgency is. It's like I made a decision and now I just want to breeze through it and then deal with whatever I find. I can put my attorney on it and see what he can find?" She said.

"Whichever way you want to do it, I support you a hundred percent." I said as I grabbed her hand and pulled her off the swing.

We walked back to the shelter making small talk about the beauty of the day.

❧

Two days later, it didn't seem like two days had passed. We had gone back to the shelter and Sam had undertaken a new project to attempt to get back on course right after calling Dean and asking him to overnight the materials. He had missed the mail out time, so it would be the following day that he would mail it out. I had gone back to the house and prepared dinner and gotten a special evening planned for Samantha and made love with her all night long to show her how much I loved her and to keep her mind off of things. We had talked a lot about what the response might be inside her and how she might feel and had fallen asleep fairly content that the truth would be somewhat freeing.

I got home early and was now waiting for the mail. The phone rang.

"Hello." I said.

"Is it there yet?" Samantha said.

"No, Honey," I laughed. "It's just now ten o'clock. Give it time. When are you coming home?"

"I can't concentrate and I was thinking that I might just leave here now and come home. Do you think it would be okay?" She said.

"Well, I was actually thinking. What if we called Tabrai and asked her to come over, in case we find out a city or something and well, she might know more than we do, since she's from Russia. I was just thinking..." I hesitated. I had been thinking about it all day and it seemed to me that they might give us a name and a city and some sort of community information in the report that is coming. Tabrai had come to mind as an answer to getting what information we could.

"I think that'd be great. Can you do that and I will just fill Miranda in on what I am doing and she can page me if she needs me." She said. "I love you...see you in about fifteen minutes."

"Okay." I said and hung up.

I looked through my planner and got Jenny's number at the gallery and called. After a few niceties and a quick synopsis of how their relationship was going, Jenny gave me the phone number to Tabrai's apartment.

She answered and agreed to help. We made plans to meet at noon for lunch at the house and she expressed her excitement at being able to help us out. I still found it very difficult to understand what she was saying through her thick accent.

I finished some things around the house and heard Samantha's truck pull up a few minutes later.

She came bounding through the door, nearly out of breath "Is it here yet?" She said.

"No, Sweetie, not yet. But, it should be here soon. Overnight delivery is supposed to be here by noon." I said as she fell into my arms.

She kissed me and pushed towards the couch. This was one of my most favorite things, when she was on a mission to seduce me. Her lips burned along mine as she kissed me and began unbuttoning my shirt. She found my skin and brushed against it lightly. She was starting to move down my body with kisses when the doorbell rang.

She jumped off me quicker than a bunny and was at the door. I couldn't even get my blouse buttoned before she had the door wide open and was accepting the package.

She turned to me with an expression I had never seen before as she closed the door. "What do I do now?" She said.

I had prepared myself for this; it seemed such a monumental

event in someone's life, finding out who her birthmother was. I patted the couch next to me. "Come, sit with me and we will do this together." I said.

"I can't do it." She walked from the room.

"Oh, shit." I said under my breath as I followed her into the bedroom.

I walked into the doorway and leaned on the doorjamb. "Hon, I know this is hard. You can put it away for now, if you want. It doesn't have to be done right now. You can put it away for years. It doesn't matter, when you are ready then you can do it...and until then, you have the papers at your disposal." I said. I didn't want to move to her, but to give her the space she needed.

She had thrown herself face down on the bed. I couldn't see her face. I didn't know if I should go to her or leave her alone.

She began to cry softly, her chest heaving and her body shaking.

I moved to the bed and sat beside her gently, "Honey, please talk to me." I hesitated. "It's as simple as this, Sam...you aren't probably going to find out anything more than a name and a place of birth. There probably isn't all that much in the paperwork. Most adoptions that are closed in this manner really don't give you all that much information. We can search from here, but really all you are going to get is a name," I spoke very softly, "and a location. You can do this Sam."

She cried softly. I stroked her hair and just let her lay. I had no idea what to say to her and I really tried to put myself in her place a couple of times and I didn't know what to do.

The doorbell rang. I looked at my watch and realized the time had gotten away from me; it was almost noon.

"Sam, that's Tabrai, do you want me to send her home or let her help us out? I can do whatever you want me to do." I said.

She sat up and wiped her tears off with the back of her hand. I hated seeing her upset. She was like a child, wiping away the tears from immediately swollen eyes.

"I can do it. I'm just afraid. I'll meet you in the kitchen; let me go freshen up a little bit. Will you just hold my hand?" She gazed at me intently.

"Of course I will." I smiled. I left the room and answered the door. It still amazed me that they resembled each other so much.

"Hi there, come on in, Tabrai." I said.

We moved into the kitchen and I poured the tea that I had simmering on the stove and sat down with Tabrai.

"I think Sam will be here in a few moments. She had a couple of things to do before she could come sit with us." I said.

"What do you like help with?" She said.

"Well, at this point, I'm not sure. Sam will have to tell you. Let me check on her real quick, I'll be right back." I said and left the room to find Sam.

I found Sam in the bathroom, sitting on the steps to the tub, reading the paperwork. She didn't hear me knock lightly, but the door opened enough that I could see her. She was reading intently. I started to back out of the room quietly, but she saw me.

"Come in." She looked up and placed the papers in her lap. "I read it." Her eyes were bright and read like a book; she had handled it well and was okay.

"Good, Honey. I am proud of you. Now what?" I said.

"Her name is Yelena Markov, and she was a Russian ballet dancer. She was with the Russian National Ballet Company when she was fifteen; she had me right after that. She was only sixteen when I was born." She was starry eyed. "Yelena...What a pretty name, huh?"

"Yeah, Sammie, it's a beautiful name. Tabrai is here. Would you like to share that with her? Maybe she knows something about how we might be able to get a hold of information. Do you want to get any information?" I was afraid to ask too much, she had been pretty wishy-washy all through this ordeal.

"I think so, maybe knowing would be a good thing? I think I would like to get as much as I can. It feels better since I know something." She said as she got up and started moving towards me.

"That sounds good." I took her hand and gave her a quick kiss and we moved towards the kitchen.

"Thank you for coming, Tabrai. I really appreciate this, I truly do." Sam said as she sat down at the table and laid the papers down.

Sam looked at me to continue for her. "We have a packet of information here that tells what is available to Sam. We know nothing about Russia or how we might find a Russian citizen. So, can we share with you what we have and see what we can do?" I said.

"Sure. It's fine." Tabrai said, laying her head in her hands to hear what we had by way of information.

"I guess you can just read it. It's an information sheet, it's very simple." Sam said and handed the paper to Tabrai.

She slid the papers across the table and turned to me and said, "Do you think that we could possibly find her now? I mean, what are the chances?"

"I...I know her." Tabrai said softly.

It didn't register for me immediately. I had listened to what Samantha had said. It didn't hit me that Tabrai had said what she did until Sam looked at her with astonishment.

"What do you mean? You know her?" She said so softly that I could barely make it out.

Tabrai was just shaking her head. She kept reading the paper, turning pages; there were three in all, until she was done. No one said anything. The silence was immense. I could hear the clock ticking on the wall as I watched Tabrai read and Samantha grabbed my hand hard and squeezed.

When Tabrai finished she looked up. Amazingly so, she and Sam had the exact same expression on their faces; I looked from one to the other. The color of their eyes was so similar that looking at Tabrai was almost comfortable for me. They didn't have the same haircut, or the same hair color, but it was close enough that it was eerie.

"She is my mother's sister." Again deafening silence after Tabrai's words.

The papers fell to the table as the two of them looked at each other. Sam let go of my hand and put her hands in her lap. Her face had no recognized expression on it.

"Are you okay, Sammie?" I asked.

She and Tabrai were staring at each other. She didn't even hear me.

I didn't know what to do. It was very uncomfortable sitting in the room with them staring at each other, neither moving nor speaking. It was more than five minutes. The clock kept ticking an endless, "Tick, Tick. Tick…"

Finally Tabrai spoke again, "Yelena is my mother's sister. She was a ballet dancer in Russian Ballet Company, that is all Momma ever said. Her sister left when young, she couldn't live with her pain. I never knew what her pain was. Momma has pictures of them dancing together. She gets cards a couple of times a year, no return address. She hope of one day seeing sister again. I don't know how you would get a hold of her; she is an artist, like me. She doesn't have job. She lives on the move, never staying in same place long according to letters. She is happy and healthy and doing well with her painting. One time, I tried to find her for Momma by calling all the art galleries I knew and no one knew of her work. She must use another name professionally. I don't know what to say…"

"Okay." Sam said. "Okay, I think I understand. So there is no way to find her?"

I jumped in, "You found something, Sam. Tabrai is your cousin and her mother is your aunt. You found that, you found family, Sweetheart."

For the first time Samantha registered what was going on. The tears began to stream down her face. Tabrai was not as emotional, but sat still staring at Samantha. No one spoke

Chapter Fifteen

The budget for the next year entailed so many changes for the better. I had surpassed the goals that Samantha had sat on the budget and she and I had made plans to increase the size of the shelter, to buy more property, build administrative offices and two more shelter homes were to be purchased. We had looked at several properties on our free weekends and had fallen in love with two of them. Sam spent her work time educating and supporting the women of the center along with the community and getting to know Tabrai as much as possible. They had developed a bond that was sincere, true and meaningful.

Sam had been asked to give a large seminar in Los Angeles the coming spring and had accepted immediately. It was a huge honor. She was blossoming before my eyes. The woman had become my world. I still had not said the words 'I love you' to her. I was thinking about that so much lately. I wanted it to be so special. We had not spoken of our future since the day of the carriage ride. Our lives had just fallen into a wonderful place.

The phone rang. It was before office hours, only seven o'clock in the morning. Samantha had been called into the shelter at four-thirty that morning and I had decided to come in and finish up my work so that we could leave for Gram's early.

"Hello, this is Abigail, may I help you, please?" I answered.

"Hey Abby, how are you?" I hadn't heard from Desiree in weeks.

"I'm just peachy, Des. How are you? Jenny?" I sang. I missed talking to Desiree.

"We're great, things are going much better. The counseling

wasn't a bad idea, as much as I hate to admit it, it's really helped. I called, because I wanted to catch you before you left for the holiday." She said. "I spoke to Julia and have some news. She told me I could call you, if I wanted. She got all the paperwork you provided and presented it to your former employers attorney late last week." She said.

I had given Desiree and Julia the go-ahead to take my former employer to court for wrongful termination. And, it had taken three weeks to prepare the paperwork they wanted for the case. I had given them detailed accounts of all the happenings and retained them for the purposes of getting my retirement account back. I wanted to know that my hard work was not in vein and that Samantha and I could count on that later. So, I had worked with Des and Julia and we were making an offer to my former employer before filing the case in court.

Desiree had described the plan for me, outlined the negotiation process and said that we needed to get the ball rolling, so that if they did not accept we could employ the court system to our aid before the first of the year. Her election had been successful and she started her term after the first of the year.

"Abby, they gave us a settlement. Are you sitting down Darling? Sit down if you aren't" Des knew me better than myself.

"Yes, of course I am. How bad is it? Do I have to accept it? What if we go ahead and take it to court?" I was rambling. I didn't want to lose my retirement.

"ABBY!!!! Listen to me a moment..." She was laughing. "Geez, I hate when you do that. You always think the worst. Who do you think you are working with? They bought us off on a settlement when Julia walked into his office, tossed our proposal on the table and told him what we would do if he didn't accept. He bought it. Hook, Line and Sinker, Darlin. You won!!!"

"I won." I stopped and thought. "They bought it that easy? How did you do that? I've seen their attorney's squash people. What did I get Desiree?" I was excited now.

I probably just got my retirement back. But, that would be fine.

"Well, you got your entire retirement account. It will be rolled over and you will lose nothing. And, Julia went out on a limb. She decided that we would sue them for your earning potential due to their negligence in speaking before the staff and slandering your good name in that meeting. She asked for...you ready for this Abby? This woman has balls of steel," She was laughing.

"Shit Desiree...quit teasing me...what????" I said. "Abby, they gave us $300,000 in retribution." Desiree didn't say anything further.

"Oh My God, you are kidding, right?" I said. There is no way Julia got that much money out of them. That was almost two years my salary. How did she swing that?

"Okay, what did she tell them, Des? It has to be good." I was ready to jump up and down, but I had to hear what she did to get it first. This was going to be the best holiday.

"Well, she sort of mentioned that case she won last year, you remember, the one where Dyan was fired for being gay. She insinuated there might have been a rumor circulating that you were a lesbian and if that was the case...she was going after them with everything they were worth. They signed immediately after that Abby. She said it was hysterical, even Julia couldn't believe it. She thought maybe they would give you some cash retribution, but never the whole thing. You owe that woman dinner." She was laughing now and I joined her.

It was amazing. Julia had such a reputation, but this was the best. We talked for a few more moments and then closed the conversation, I had wanted to call Samantha and tell her. We wished each other a happy holiday and left it at that.

I picked up the phone to dial Sam, but decided this was too good to phone her. I finished up what I was doing, with a huge smile on my face and jetted out the door. The office would be fine until we got back on Monday. We had twelve hours to drive to Gram's and it was getting on, we wanted to get there before it was too late tonight.

Samantha was packing the truck; we had packed our bags last night, right before we made love.

She had to be tired; she had been called into the shelter not a half-hour after we went to sleep. I pulled up just in time to help her load the truck.

I rushed out of the car, bounding up the drive. "Baby, I have news!!!!"

She stopped in her tracks and dropped the bags and we moved towards each other. I never got tired of looking at her. I kissed her, right there in her yard.

"We won...we won. Desiree called and we won, Babe. I got my retirement account back and I also got $300,000 in settlement." Sam held me at arms length.

"You have to be kidding, Abby...$300,000 in settlement. We hadn't asked for that?"

I told her the whole story as we loaded the truck. We didn't need to take a lot, but Samantha had packed every outfit and pair of shoes she owned. I laughed. She was so bad. Everywhere we had gone, it had been a debate over which shoes I liked best. Even though I never really picked, she always came away with my favorite. We were light of spirit, that's for sure. We never talked about it as far as it being our retirement account, but we both knew it was. I knew how she felt; she told me she loved me a lot. But, I just couldn't find the right time. It seemed like every time I tried to say it, she would kiss my words away. And, I had not gotten the chance.

I had even planned it one night. I had thought about it all day. But, no, when it got time...she fell asleep. She had been exhausted. When I had finished work, I went from her, or now "our" office, back to the bedroom, where she had been reading cases and found her asleep. So, I hadn't pressed the issue.

We finished up the packing of the truck and made sure we had everything. I called Gram and told her we were on our way. She was excited to meet Samantha. I hadn't told the rest of my family she was coming. I was a little worried. My family was not very accepting in the past. So, I had warned Sam and we had decided that it was no big deal. We wanted to share it and I wanted to show her my world. I would share my entire life with her.

We started out our journey, by loading the CD player and Samantha getting pillows and blankets ready so that she could sleep. The CD player bellowed the music we had chosen and she laid a pillow on my lap, while I drove. We headed out of town.

It was nine o'clock; we were right on time. I had made this drive many times, it took almost twelve hours, if you stopped and ate once and kept the other breaks to a minimum.

"This is our first trip, did you realize that?" She asked.

Gram had called me one night while we were at my house about a month ago. Sam answered the phone. Immediately Gram wanted to know who Samantha was. Sam didn't know not to tell her. I was standing in the kitchen and had heard the whole conversation. I had never even been called to the phone. I could hear my grandmother on the other end. She was so demure, petite, and down right to the point.

Gram had said, "Who is this and what are you doing at Abby's house? I know there is no room for another woman in her life; I am all she can handle." and she had laughed.

Samantha told her that she was my cleaning lady and she was just taking her pay out in trade, that I was making her dinner. Grandmother had instantly liked her. I had mentioned to Sam that Gram had an amazing sense of humor, and she had played it to perfection. I adored Samantha's courage and zest. So had grandmother. Gram had invited us both down for Thanksgiving weekend and Sam had accepted for us both. And that is how this all came about.

About three hours into the trip, my auburn angel awoke. She snuggled up close to me and caressed my arm. She spoke as she stretched, "Hi, Darling."

I stroked her hair, pushed it gently behind her ear, "Hi, Baby...sleep well?"

Her reply was so adorable, "Uh huh, I did. But, I missed

you. I dreamt about you again. You were walking toward me again, but couldn't go any father and I had to really work to get to you. It was like I was in quicksand or something."

She had been having this dream on and off for about a month.

"Awww, Honey. I'm sorry. You're just tired. I'm right here, not going anywhere." I tried to reassure her.

I was going nowhere. She had captivated me. I had worried about that dream though. She was very clingy after she had it, the whole next day, until she was home with me again.

She had made life so great for me. Each morning there were notes and treats and packages sent to my office. One afternoon, six-dozen roses were delivered to me, all from different florists, each one with a different note from her, in her handwriting. She had said later that evening, that every time she had gone past a florist, she stopped and ordered, because she missed me so much. Each dozen had a white rose in the middle, a reverse of the very first ones I gave her. She was special, very special, and I knew it.

She began to talk as I drove, "Last night was pretty rough. We got a new client in and I had to go pick her up at the hospital. She had been beaten pretty badly by her husband. I had to get her to the shelter without him knowing, he was at the hospital and wouldn't leave her alone. I couldn't get him arrested, because he was the one who brought her in. They let him stand by as they took care of her and you could just see the fear in her eyes. When I showed up, it was a mess. They made him leave the room so that I could talk to her and he didn't like that one bit. The police had to escort him out and he called me all kinds of names and said I was there to take her away from him." She sighed and moved to a more comfortable position.

"As soon as the courts opened this morning, Miranda had to take Denise, that's her name, down to get a restraining order issued. Abby, it's a mess; I have a bad feeling about this one. Sometimes I don't understand the women. I had to literally yank this woman out of the hospital and yet when I talked to her about the restraining order, she stood looking at me like I was making her order it. I had to tell her it was her decision, for her protection. She actually asked me what I would do if I were her. I explained to her, if someone beat me up so badly that I was bleeding, my face looked like I was a boxer and my ribs were broken, I might just have to save my life. She didn't understand, Abby. I was lucky; I got out before mine convinced me that she was all that would want me. Denise swears that no one else will have her, so she has to go back. We talked most of the night about it, about the cycle of abuse. She understood, I thought. I was just frustrated. To see her so easily swayed so quickly after being beaten, Abby, she will be a likely candidate to go back. Next time she might not be so lucky." Samantha sighed again.

I knew what she meant. I had talked on the crisis line so many times to women who were in situations that were terribly unsafe. They told me that all they had to do was get through the moment that their abuser would change. And, they were right for the most part. The cycle of abuse was usually consistent. Once they got beaten, or verbally abused severely, they could count on an apology and the cycle beginning again, it was circular. You had the building stage, where things were nice, sometimes referred to as 'euphoric' even; then there was the eggshell stage, where things were getting tense; the final stage was the breaking point. Many deaths had resulted in the final stage. Women and children, for the most part, were the ones who suffered. Usually there was drinking involved and well, it was devastating. It was hard to leave, because the next stage was where the abuser made up for all that they had done, everything was their fault and they were going to change. Rarely did that occur, but rather, the abuse cycle would start again.

On the crisis lines, we could only point out the obvious and help the women find resources to help them out. Because much of the time, there was alcohol involved, there were a lot of women who couldn't feed their children, didn't have money to run their households, and more. We merely offered resources and the chance for a change if they wanted to leave the situation and had nowhere to go. I had seen exactly what Sam was talking about. There was nothing you could do, but make them see where they were and where they were possibly going, lend a loving ear and be compassionate for their situation. For me, it was enough knowing how I had not seen the situation until I was out of it for a long time. Sam and I had spoken of it many times, how hard it was for us to leave. Our situations were a little different, but similar in the sense that you didn't see it until you were in so deep, the control was so all-encompassing that you couldn't really get out. You just didn't see; it was like being brainwashed.

"Abby, I have a bad feeling about this one. He was there last night at the hospital waiting, when we left he acted like he would follow us. The police took us to the station on my request. He scared me, because he didn't make a scene, he was too calm after having been so belligerent."

She was worried; I could see it.

She continued, moving closer to me, snuggling in, "I left both our pager numbers and your grandmother's number for them to call, if they need to."

That should make her feel better, at least she knew that Miranda and Shelby would call if they needed and the police were so quick to get to the shelter if there was the slightest disturbance.

"Oh, Abby, guess what else?" she became excited as she spoke, rising to a sitting position in her chair, getting comfortable, "Tommy and his mom were leaving the shelter today. They were going to go stay with family for Thanksgiving. She has a job interview there on Friday. Her aunt picked them up while I was there, and she seemed really nice. Tommy seemed to be pleased. They will be back on Saturday morning, but seemed really excited to go. If she gets the job, the aunt said they could stay with them until they got settled into an apartment." She smiled.

I knew how much Tommy meant to both of us. It was good to see people move on from the shelter without fear. Tommy and his mother had come such a long way since they had entered the shelter. They had nothing and now they had some potential.

"Hey, Sammie. What are we going to do with the money?" I had just now thought about the fact that I was going to pay off all my bills and have money left over.

Sam grinned, "What do you think? It's really your money, what do you want to do?" She was being coy.

"My money, huh? Well, I thought I might share it with you. I don't know. We want for nothing, I thank God daily. I have nothing lacking in my life. I thought about maybe investing at least half of it in an ILA, and then if we needed it, we would still have it, it would be liquid. We have the tickets to the Bahamas, if you still want me to go," I grinned, and she acted like she was hitting me.

"What do you think? Is there anything that we might do?" She looked out the window on her side, she was thinking.

I had begun to realize when she was in thought. I knew she was contemplating her answer, how she would word it.

"Say it like you think it, Samantha. It's easier to understand anyway."

She looked at me. "Abby, we are cruising at..." she looked at the speedometer, "over 80 mph and you can't jump out, so I am going to take a chance here."

She moved closer to me so that she could lay her head on my shoulder. I obliged, by putting my arm around her shoulder and pulling her closer.

She began again, "I would like to sell both our houses and maybe build a house together some day. I loved looking at houses with you for the shelter. Wasn't that fun? And then we would discuss how we liked certain features, but didn't like others. And, well, the last day we looked, when we were looking at the house on Peoria Street, the one we liked so much, I thought, wouldn't it be great if we were buying a house together, just you and I?" She didn't look at me, but rather, just snuggled up with me.

"It's a wonderful thought, Sam. I like it. When the money comes through, maybe we could start planning or looking. It takes so long to build; maybe we could draw up some plans and have someone look at them, that sounds great."

I kissed her forehead. We really didn't talk much after that; she fell back asleep. I stopped around two o'clock and grabbed us something to eat, while Samantha stayed asleep in the truck. I splashed some water on my face and felt more refreshed; we were almost half way there. I was really looking forward to seeing Gram. She is the only one who acted like I wasn't a lesbian, and treated my girlfriends with more respect than anyone else. She would love Samantha.

I knew she would have my very own pan of home made macaroni and cheese, she always did. I missed my family sometimes. .

Sam woke up a couple of hours before we arrived and she put her makeup back on in the truck rearview mirror. We stopped and got her something to eat and she freshened up. We took a little walk, hand-in-hand, along the row of stores and restaurants that we stopped at and stretched our legs. And, then we were back on the road. I was ready to be there.

Samantha drove the rest of the way and I lay in her lap. I sang to her with CD's and made fun of half the songs, making up my own silly words. We had fun. Finally, we pulled up at Gram's.

"There it is." I pointed out. "My mom's car's there already, so we aren't going to be able to talk to Gram alone, something I was actually looking forward to. I wanted you to feel at home before meeting the un-accepting side of my family. But, "I explained to her, "before we go inside remember that I don't care how they feel. I am in charge of my feelings. Deal?"

She nodded.

At the door, Gram greeted us with hugs and kisses. She acted as if Samantha had been one of the family for years. Her house was small, so the moment we walked in, we were in front of everyone. Mom, my brother, my sister-in-law, my niece and Gram were all there.

Everyone rushed to hug me, leaving Samantha to stand holding Gram's hand. My mom started in right away telling me things about "life at home." Samantha caught my glimpse as I said; "Here we go" without saying anything.

After the initial shock wore off and I was able to break

away for a moment, about twenty minutes later. I went to Sam. Gram had taken her aside and they were making a dessert. They had waited supper for us and it smelled wonderful. I went to the kitchen to help.

I walked up behind Gram and hugged her close, "What goodies did you make for me, Grammy?"

"What makes you think I would make anything special for you?" she bellowed.

She was a small woman. I had always thought her hair was so cool, because she never grayed. Little did I know this eighty-year-old woman did not have jet-black hair? It was a huge blow to me, when I figured it out at about nineteen. I couldn't believe it when I found out she died her hair.

Samantha smiled at me as she stirred what she was told and fetched when she was told. She looked like she was having fun. Gram kept her busy as my mom and brother monopolized my attention until dinner.

Dinner was uneventful and afterwards, we all played cards. I played footsie with Samantha under the table, but kept it to a real minimum. My brother told of his new career, real estate, and we found ourselves asking him a lot of questions about building or buying. He was adamant about buying, due to the nature of construction these days.

"They can get away with cheaper products and the houses aren't as well made." He said, "Definitely buy. Find an older home, with a solid foundation and remodel. I have seen people do some fabulous things."

We agreed with his points.

"Are you thinking about buying again, Abby?" He said.

I shook my head, told them about the news of the day and my retirement account and we opened a bottle of wine and celebrated. My sister-in-law made toast after toast to us, as if she were trying to "out" us at the table, but we all took it in stride and had fun.

We played more cards, ate snacks, drank wine and just enjoyed each other's company.

It was Tuesday night. The next day, we had planned to take Gram Christmas shopping...just Samantha and I. The plans changed a little, because Mother and my brother had to work and Cheyenne and my sister-in-law were going to accompany us. It sounded like fun.

We broke up and scattered in different directions about eleven o'clock, Samantha and I staying at Gram house. My mother was a bit upset, because I wasn't staying with her, but she hadn't invited Samantha. It was her only stab at us, but I blew it off even though it still hurt.

Samantha knew it. As soon as she left, Sam asked, "Are you okay?"

"I'm used to it. Honey, it just hurts. They can't welcome my life into theirs, makes me feel like an outsider." I tried to blow it off the best I could; tomorrow was another day. We sat and talked to Gram for a while. She was getting tired and so was I.

"Gram, why don't you go to bed? Sam and I can put everything up. We don't mind. I'd like another glass of wine and to just relax anyway." I said.

Sam nodded in agreement. Gram wasn't about to argue. She kissed us both and gave us loving hugs and scooted away into her room. We were staying in the guest room.

We sat in the dining room at my grandmother's and I got out old photo albums. We held hands and went through the albums and I showed her family pictures. On the third page, was a picture of my father when he was in the Army.

Sam placed her fingers on his picture as if she had known him and said, "I wish I could have met him, Abby. He sounds like such a nice guy." She squeezed and smiled.

"I have wished that many times, it's hard not having him around on the holidays. I'm getting a little tired, do you mind if we lay in the living room and finish looking?" I said.

We moved to the living room and laid some pillows down and finished looking at pictures. I showed her my little brother; he was killed on a motorcycle when he was twenty. He was my best friend." I touched his picture and lovingly remembered his friendship to me.

It was kind of neat lying in my Gram's house, remembering old times, telling Sam about them and just reminiscing.

"My holidays consisted of my family trying to impress people. My mom would sneak up to see me just to say happy holidays, while I was upstairs in my room, alone, unless beckoned down to make an impression. I had one friend, the cleaning woman, Martha. She would leave me little bits of her family holiday cheer, hidden away from my parents. I really hadn't had much of a family, even though I truly did love mother."

It seems as if the one thing I had and could not give her or share with her, was my family. And that made me angry to an extent, because it wasn't that I wasn't willing, but that my family wasn't. I couldn't tell her that.

Sam was pretty much awake, because she had slept so much on the road, but I was exhausted. As she talked about the pictures, asking questions and the likes, I fell asleep on the floor.

She must have kept looking. There were books scattered all over the floor in the morning, with Sam laying asleep on one in particular. She had been looking at a scrapbook that my grandmother had apparently made of me. It had all my college clippings, my high school awards and pictures. It was something I had never seen before.

I went to kiss Sam and saw myself at regional softball tournament, winning MVP and Samantha asleep on my picture.

I leaned over and kissed her on the cheek and said, "I love you, Samantha. More than you could possibly know."

I didn't know if she heard me or not, she stirred just for a moment, but fell back asleep as I slid the book out of her grasp and slid a pillow underneath her head. I went to the couch and got a throw and covered her, tucked her in and went into the kitchen.

Gram had been up for hours. It was nearly nine o'clock.

"Morning Gram," I kissed her cheek.

"Well, good morning Miss Abigail. Sleep all the day on my living room carpet?" She smiled.

"Sorry Grammy, we fell asleep. I was pretty tired." I said.

"Oh, little one, I know. I was up early this morning and I saw you both in there. Abigail, I just wanna say this once. Never again to be mentioned. Is that understood?" She was militant in her attitude; she looked me square in the eye.

Uh oh.... what now? I wasn't sure I wanted to hear this. It sounded like one of her speeches was coming and I hadn't had one of those in years.

"Sure Grammy, you know you can trust me." I said.

She began the speech, "I am telling you that your happiness is very important to me, Abigail. I haven't seen you this happy in about ten years, if not longer. I'm not getting any younger and I want some grandkids. And, well, little Cheyenne is the only child your brother will be having," she spoke the truth, they had tried for a long time and finally been blessed, but there would be no more children from them.

Grandma continued, very stern in her manner, but looking me square, "I want some little red headed children. It has always been a dream of mine," she stopped speaking as we heard Samantha coming into the room.

Sam caught us both silent and must have felt awkward. "Uh, morning, I can go into the other room." as she turned back around.

"Nonsense child, get in here with Abigail. You need to hear this too." she was motioning for Sam to come stand by me.

Sam did as she was told and came to stand beside me, questioning me with her eyes as she moved past grandmother. We both stood and listened to Gram as she spoke to both of us now.

"I was telling Abigail, I want some red headed babies. I've always known that I needed some red headed babies in this family. My mother was red headed." She spoke as she reached for Samantha's hair. "Samantha, she had hair almost like yours, exact color, same thickness, very nice. I want some babies." She pouted. "The two of you are going to give them to me."

I was astounded. I was sitting here listening to my grandmother tell me that my girlfriend and I were to give her babies. And, red headed babies at that, meaning they were to come from Samantha. My hair had tints of red, but was not red. The way that she touched Samantha's hair, it was like she was remembering. She had a far off look.

She spoke again, "I know you have trouble in this life, but I won't stand for it here in my house. Abby, Sam and I sat up after you went to bed last night and we talked."

She looked at Sam and Sam nodded okay as she spoke again, "We talked about all this and it's okay with her. I want you to do whatever it is you need to do, to give me my family. I am not sure what you Lebanese do, but I am sure that you know how to get me my babies. Now, we will never speak of this again. I know your mother has a real problem with you being Lebanese...but, well," she stomped her foot, "I like Samantha, Abigail, and you better be nice to her. We are done, now take me shopping so I can get my Christmas started."

We were roaring with laughter. Gram thought her joke about me being nice to Samantha was a real hit. I couldn't bear to correct her back to lesbian.... Lebanese would have to do.

We showered quickly and dressed as fast. Gram would not stand for being stood up. We dressed in slacks and blouses, comfortable shoes and I put on a sweater. We headed to the mall with Gram to "start her Christmas." On the way, we picked up my sister-in-law and Cheyenne and when Gram insisted on going to the door after them we wanted to argue but couldn't. We almost had to have a tow truck lift her into the Rodeo, but would she listen?

I took the opportunity to turn quickly to Samantha, who was in the back seat, "What in the world went on last night, Darlin?" She knew what I meant.

She had the biggest smile I had seen so far on her face, her eyes lit up.

She said, "Your grandmother pulled me back into the

kitchen, pinned me against the wall and made me tell her about us. She wanted to know everything, how we met, who asked who what, where we lived, what I did for a career, she third degreed me. I thought she was going to hook up the lamp and draw it to my face. She was adamant, yet she was so loving as she did it. I told her everything, Abby; she wanted me to. She gave me this." She held up a gold medallion.

I was stunned, I just looked at her; it was plain, like the one on my statuette.

Samantha continued, "She told me that she got this in W.W.I, that her brother brought it back to her and she wanted me to have it and it was to be passed down to our children. I nearly fell off my chair, Abigail. Why me? Why didn't she give it to you?"

We saw Gram coming down the sidewalk and like children had to stop talking. "I will talk to her later, don't worry, she likes you and she is the boss. No one tells her what to do, she is wise, always has been, there's a reason, even if we don't know it. Don't worry your pretty head." I said, as Gram opened the door.

"That is the slowest set of girls I have ever seen." She was impatient and Lisa and Cheyenne were not hurrying quite quick enough, but finally got themselves situated in the back with Sam and Gram hoisted herself into the truck; we were off to shop.

The day was long and tedious. I had never looked at so many of the same things to price them before. I didn't realize how hard it was living on a fixed income. Gram had to select each present with the greatest of care. Sam and I had talked about it, while Gram was shopping; we were giving her money for Christmas and a big screen TV with built in VCR. It was all luxury, but she complained about not being able to see her soap opera's.

We were having the item delivered that day; Samantha took my credit card and bought the TV, while I helped Gram pick out Samantha's Christmas present. She got Samantha a jewelry box; it was very nice. She said she had a ring that she wanted to put in it too. Our family was going to do our Christmas over

Thanksgiving, because my brother was going to Phoenix and Sam and I were going to the Bahamas. So, we were preparing.

I hadn't gotten Sam anything. I had been thinking about it for a long time and just didn't know what to give her. I asked Gram, "What could I get for Samantha?"

She looked at me, "I have just the thing Abigail, don't you worry, she is taken care of." and that was that.

I knew it would be special and figured I could pick up something for her when we got home. Her and I would have our Christmas later anyway.

Sam came back, "Mission accomplished. I got a nice one for her. It'll look great in her house and it matches her walnut tables. It was on sale too." She was so efficient.

"Thanks Samantha," I smiled.

After that, we went and had lunch and talked about old times. Mostly we talked about what a dork I was growing up. My grandmother told us all how stupid I was as a kid; her memory sure wasn't going. Cheyenne hardly left Samantha's side. She held her hand and talked to Sam. We ate and laughed. My most embarrassing moments revealed to all.

We dropped Lisa and Cheyenne off at the house and they were going to wrap presents and then meet us at Gram's later. We stopped by the store and bought all we needed for Sam and I to make manicotti for dinner. We had a good time trying to make sure that Gram would eat it. She was as picky as I. So, with groceries in tow, we had about ten minutes to get back to the house, before the deliverymen were to be delivering the gift for Gram. We rushed back with Gram swearing she would never ride with me again. We all laughed.

We got home just after the deliverymen. Gram knew immediately that we had done something and started telling us that she hoped that this wasn't for her. She had a small smile peeking out though and we both saw it. The guys sat everything up and Gram didn't leave her chair the rest of the afternoon, but bellowed out commands from there for us in the kitchen; she was loving it. She decided she needed a remote that could hunt for tapes for her and she would never have to move. I thought of Samantha's handy-dandy remote.

The rest of the family showed up. We ate the manicotti and drank wine and talked about what we were all doing in our lives. It was actually very nice. My mom was a peach. She talked about work and how she was feeling. It was a real family moment. We then moved to the living room for our family Christmas.

We exchanged gifts. My brother and I had gone together and gotten my mother a computer. He had suggested it month's prior and it had already been taken care of. Greg got Lisa a new ring, diamond and ruby and she was moved to tears. She got him a new table saw, the big stud with his power tools. And little Cheyenne raked it in. She got dolls and a puppy, she got books and crayons, and clothing and we got her a CD player and some CD's. My brother was taken aback, but we explained to him that any four year old could get into music and if she had help, would respect her gift and she nodded in agreement. She hugged our necks and had to try it out. Mom got her a new desk for her room and Gram got her a little necklace. It was dainty and sweet, just like Cheyenne she said.

I got a new computer case from my brother's family, a sweater from my mother and some perfume I would never use. From Gram, I got a necklace. It was a black pearl caged in gold. We all picked up the ripped paper; I filled wine glasses and Gram called me to her room.

She pulled from her jewelry box a diamond ring. I knew the ring well, I had seen her wear it my whole life. It was her wedding ring.

"Abigail, you are the oldest grandchild. I'd always intended for you to wear this ring when you got married. I guess that I might have to change that perception," she looked at me with the sweetest face, "please take this ring, Abby."

She placed it in my hand and folded my fingers around it as she held my hand in hers. "Abby, do you love her?"

I couldn't believe I was standing her talking to my grandmother like this. "Gram, I have only known Samantha for a couple of months. I do love her. I love her like I have known her forever. But I don't know if I should love her so quickly." I said.

My grandmother took her hands from mine and placed them on my shoulders. "Abby, you have always lived with your head instead of your heart. Ever since your daddy died, you've been a thinker. What does your heart tell you, child? God gave you a heart for a reason. He made you see things in certain people and not in others, so you would know them when you got to them. Can you live without her?"

I knew what she was saying, "No, Grandmother, if something were to happen to her, I wouldn't want to. I love her very much...with all my heart."

Gram hugged me close and kissed my cheek. "Take the ring Abigail and when the moment is right, you ask her for forever... just like your grandfather did for me. There is something about that girl. She's part of this family and I told her about that last night. We had a good talk. She loves you, Abigail, pure and honestly, she loves you."

She patted my back as we turned to walk back into the living room; I tucked the ring in my pocket. I would give it to her in the Bahamas; that would be very special.

We finished the night as the night prior, with family and games, a lot of stories and some laughter. Mom was great. I sat by her the rest of the night and held her hand.

She talked about my brother, Jeff, and she talked of my father and I knew how much she missed them. But, all was good and Mom ended up staying at Gram's with us. She stayed in the guest room and Sam and I stayed in the living room again.

We didn't fall asleep on the floor; we kissed for hours.

"I'm sorry that I didn't get you a present. I knew we were having Christmas together later. But, now I wish I would have gotten you something small." She said.

"Don't worry about it. I know you love me and that's all that I care about." I said as I kissed her and we tried to make love quietly on the floor, in all our clothes.

❧

Thanksgiving day was filled with food and laughter and other people. Gram had friend's stop by, our aunt and uncle came in with their two boys, and my two cousins came. It was a house full of people, everyone talking and catching up. Sam stayed by my side the whole day. I knew it was a little overwhelming for her, but she did great. I saw her sneak away once and followed her shortly after outside.

"Are you okay?" I asked.

"Yes. I just get a little overwhelmed. I have never had family before. It's kind of different. I am used to spending holidays at the shelter or alone. Lauren didn't allow me to come, her family didn't know about her." She said.

"Let's walk. I'll show you my neighborhood." I said, wanting to spend some time alone with her so that she was comfortable.

We took a walk and I showed her the church that I grew up in and we went into the Chapel and prayed together. It was something we'd never done. I felt it was the closest that we had ever been. We held hands and gave thanks for what we had been given, the gift of love and family and the ability to share it together.

"I haven't ever done that with anyone before," she said as we walked out of the church. "Praying is so personal. But, it felt very easy. You are easy."

"This is how it's supposed to be, ya know?" I said. I wanted to tell her I loved her. But, I didn't know how to do it. It didn't seem special enough to just say it while we were walking, we couldn't really stop and just be in the moment. I wanted to be able to kiss her when I said it. In my own mind I was starting to doubt whether or not I could do it. I knew I loved her, I just couldn't say it.

When we got back to Gram's we helped clean up. Everyone had quieted down and all was well. We had all picked some movies and found out just how wonderful Grams new present was.

As she went to get her video out and put it in the VCR...she found her other surprise. I had written her a check for $25,000.

She opened the tape case and saw the check. She didn't bat an eye. She folded it up and tucked it in her little dress. On her way back to sit down, she walked to where Sam and I were sitting and smacked me on the head.

"Thank you, Abby. I really needed that," she said with a tear in her eye. She then went and sat down and we watched the movie.

We all went to bed that night quite content. We had a wonderful family time and I was looking forward to the next day, we were just going to be with Gram. Samantha and I talked a little before we went to bed, kissing and holding each other and sharing what we had found, our family. It had been a long time since I had even acknowledged my family as my own and now I got to share it with Sam.

We were awakened at three-thirty by Gram. "Samantha, Sweetie, wake up." Gram was saying softly. "Honey, you have a phone call."

Sam took the phone in the kitchen. "I understand Miranda. Calm down. Yes, I know. I will take care of it. Don't be afraid, you'll have the whole place in fear...I will be there as soon as I can get there. Give me two seconds. Call Shelby on the other line and get her in." She looked at me.

She put her hand over the receiver and then said, "I have to go back. I can fly or you can go with me and we can drive. But we need to leave now. Denise's husband found the shelter. He stood outside last night and watched all night; tonight Miranda has been watching him outside the window. He is scaling the perimeter of the shelter and she is freaking out. I have to calm her, but I need to get back, everyone is really afraid watching her look out the window at him and Denise is hysterical. She has no family to be taken to. You remember last time?"

I nodded. The last time this happened we had the police help out. We took the woman outside to a police car and they took her to a family member's after keeping her at the police station until her husband could be escorted home. We couldn't put many in jeopardy because of one client.

I said, "You do what you need to do, make plans. I'm going with you."

"Ladies. Get your things together. I will get the plane reservations squared away while you pack your things and get Myra next door to take you to the airport. She is always up all night." Gram said. "Your brother can drive your truck home. He is off until Monday."

She gave Miranda exact instructions as to what to do and told her she would be there early the next afternoon; that she felt it would be okay until then. She told Miranda to call for a fifteen minute interval drive by for the police and that if they needed anything else, to page us while we were on the road, but in the event of an emergency, to use the police first. There was nothing we could do from here. We would get on the road as soon as we could. She hung up and came to the table where Gram and I were sitting. We had said nothing.

Samantha said, "For the most part it's best to move the inhabitant associated with the problem and notify the spouse, so that they had to look elsewhere. Miranda had tried to make those arrangements for Denise to be moved, to no avail. The homeless shelter is full to overflowing. There are no staff members in town that can take her in and she has no family. It's not a good situation. Miranda described a sense of fear. Denise saw her husband outside and became extremely fearful. One of the counselors spoke to her, but it didn't help much. The shelter has a strict policy on something of this nature and so Miranda requested that the inhabitant in question not tell other inhabitants, it provokes panic. Denise freaked out and some of the other women heard what was going on and became fearful too. Now the shelter is like a fortress of scared women. They are continually looking out the windows. Miranda called the police earlier and they escorted him away. He's not in violation of the restraining order, because he stands far enough away to just watch."

I said, "He's probably letting her know that he knows where she is."

Sam's face had become drawn and I could tell she was stressing. I knew this situation could escalate and it was best that we return home.

I started to explain to Gram, "Gram, we really need to go, we are, by far, too far away to be of much help here."

She cut me off, "You two fly back. We can get you to the airport in just a short time. Gather your bags and I will call for tickets. Give me a credit card Abby and I'll take care of it. Your mother has to work tomorrow, but they can leave after she gets off work and take turns with the three of them driving and get you the truck and then drive home. She was already moving to the phone book. I was impressed.

"Samantha, is that okay with you? It's your truck." I said. She was just looking at Gram in amazement. She got up and went to Gram and put her arms around her. Samantha began sobbing. She so readily cried. Gram patted her head and comforted her.

"Gram, I have never been treated so well. I want you to know how much this has meant to me." Samantha said softly. Gram just patted and looked at me and winked.

Gram called and made arrangements. They were fine driving the truck back and then driving home. She called the airport and had a flight for us in 45 minutes. She made them aware that we would be later than the recommended check in time; they assured her that if we were there ten minutes early; we would be fine.

We gathered our bags and packed one of them with the things we would need to get home and left the others to be driven back with the truck and headed back to the kitchen. Gram had more coffee prepared and even though I wasn't a coffee drinker, it sure did smell good. I took bottled water for the trip and Sam a bottle of juice. Myra picked us up about ten minutes later.

Gram was silent. But, Samantha couldn't contain herself. "Gram, would you like to come see us sometime? We would love to have you," she spoke hopefully.

"Well, I was just thinking I might just go with the kids to take your truck back. This bad back of mine wouldn't be bothered much by it, and I *have* wanted to go somewhere. You have anything exciting down there in the big city that I might like to see?" Gram smiled at Sam.

"I think we might be able to find something. That would be great. Just let me get back and take care of this problem. I just need to move Denise and get this gentleman on his way. I will get him arrested as soon as I get there. And then we should all be fine. I just need him to make a mistake and I'll have him. After that we will do what we can to finish our holiday." she was delighted with the thought. Her smile was so beautiful.

Gram was right. I did love her with everything about me. I was beaming at Gram when she looked at me, suggesting to me that she liked Samantha more than a little bit. Myra blew the horn and we kissed Gram and away we went.

Chapter Sixteen

I was silent as I walked along the path. I thought about how long it had been, since I had any serenity in my life. Tears were streaming down my face. It really wasn't fair that one person had to go through all this torment. How could I help but be bitter? My girlfriend had just told me that day she needed space, why wouldn't I be bitter? What did that really mean, but that she was ending it. This was the beginning of the end, and on Valentine's Day. How could she do this to me today? I knew that her canceling our plans for the evening meant that she had met someone else and they would likely be sharing this evening. You would think a big strong woman like myself, emotionally fit, since I dealt with my problems, could handle this. But, I wasn't dealing well.

I felt myself nearly fall as I dropped down in the grass by the shore of the lake. I held my head in my hands, crying. I remembered all the times that I had with her and how special they were. I wept for joy and extreme sorrow; I wept for compassion of self and self-hatred. How could I have not seen this coming? Why had I not been prepared? I wept freely as dusk neared. I didn't see the pink horizon of the evening. I didn't see the sun dropping behind the lake and its sheer unabashed beauty. I missed out on the birds landing with their lovers for the evening and the songs they sang. I missed all of the good in those moments that the tears washed my soul.

"I'll never love again." I wailed. My sobbing had become audible. I heard myself weep, a mournful cry, I heard my own pain.

As I cried, softly, she touched my shoulder. She didn't

startle me, her graceful hand touching me. She patted me in comfort, the gentleness consoling me. I could not raise my head, I didn't have the strength, and I didn't care who she was. I could only weep.

She knelt beside me; like a mother she held me. In her arms, strong and secure, I whimpered. It was for or my father dying; my best friend's suicide; I missed my ex-lover's nephew we were raising before we split six years ago; losing my job because I was gay; my brother dying in a motorcycle wreck; and now this, I grieved. The pain was immense; it had been building and had burst. She softened the pain with tears for me, spilling on my shoulder from her own eyes. I didn't know why she was crying, but I felt her kindness through my pain. I felt a oneness with her.

After what seemed like hours, my sobbing subsided; still she held me. I noticed she smelled of rain, the scent that drifts to you right before a calm storm. I placed my head, heavily laden with my pain, on her chest. She stroked my hair and began to sing. Her song was soft and beautiful, her voice charming me. There was no one there but she and I. Her encouragement was spirituous. My eyes nearly swollen shut, I attempted to look at her face, her features faint. I was only inches from her, engulfed in her long, flowing, fiery, red hair, yet, I couldn't make out her features.

It was okay, she was my friend, she had to be, I thought to myself. It never occurred to me to question, who she was, in her perfection. She had brought me out of the pain; anguish I didn't think could be stopped. Prior to her relief, I truly thought that if I just lay down, I would die, it would be that easy.

Her melodic song ended. Realizing it had no words, I looked again at her face, and still no features were defined. My senses were coming back to an awareness state; I could feel her clothing beneath my face, between the two of us. She wore a dress of sorts, made of gauzy material and cream in color.

I remained in her arms, not wanting to leave the comforting place. The stroking of my hair stopped, her arms still assisting me in heartening. I was drained. She had sung without words and reached my soul. She had found me when I thought no one could. I had wanted to die, here at the lake, to just fade away, with the suffering I felt. But, here she was.

Out of the silence, she spoke, "My friend, the challenge is yours. You make this choice today and every day. You may give in; lie down and die, or you may choose to live. You think about that, here with me, in my arms of safety, before you choose, please." The softness in her voice was endearing. I took that time to think.

I thought about my niece that I loved dearly. I also thought about my brother, who made no attempt to keep in contact with me, because of my lesbian lifestyle. My mother, after losing my father, couldn't keep the family together...and then my little brother was killed, my mind drifted. I knew my family didn't understand me. My friends, they loved me dearly for what I gave them of myself. And, I had me. I couldn't lie down and die, no matter how painful it was, because they loved me. My family had been through, by far, too much already. I thought these thoughts, not speaking.

My comforter spoke again, "I am glad you see these things, Abigail. Now take them, as you take all good in your life for eternity, and live." She released me. Her arms dropping as she got up.

Still kneeling in the grass, I felt a chill as she walked away from me towards the water. As she came to the water's edge, she did not stop, but walked out onto the water never looking back. She walked across the water until I could see her no longer.

I had been in the chapel of the hospital praying for the last two hours, as I remembered this experience. I had this experience five years prior, the angel of mine coming to me. I prayed for Samantha, the woman I loved, as she lay in the coma, just doors away. I began praying, remembering the angel that had kept me alive through my pain. My pain was that bad now. Samantha was everything to me. What if she died too, I couldn't do it again?

She was in the coma, because she had been selfless. She had moved in front of Denise at the crisis shelter, three days prior. Denise's husband, furious at having had a restraining order against him, had come to kill Denise. Samantha had saved her, given her time to flee with all the other inhabitants of the shelter, by stepping in front of her and taking a blow to the head. That blow had been meant to kill Denise.

After that, he had beaten Samantha into a coma in his anger. It was such a blur to me. I had gone to the shelter with her right from the airport. The taxi had pulled up in front and we saw him then. He was just standing there, leaning against a tree. He had this look on his face as he watched us and we watched him. It was about twenty minutes to nine in the morning. The women that were in the shelter that worked were leaving and we had just entered. He broke through them and headed straight for Denise. He was like lightning. I didn't see him coming. I had gone into the office to call the police and everyone else was in the front room talking to Sam about the time off she had just taken for the Holiday. They were exchanging hugs when he came in.

I had heard the women screaming. I ran in just in time to see Samantha land on the floor and he started kicking her and pounding on her. Everyone fled out the back door; women and children were screaming in terror as they ran. I pushed through them and grabbed a golf club that was leaning against the wall. I beat the shit out of him. I don't know how he survived. I beat him until he didn't move and then I went to Samantha, where Miranda was holding her. I began checking Sam for a pulse and all, my CPR training coming in handy. She had a pulse and was breathing.

Miranda ran and called an ambulance. I spoke to Sam, as she lay in my arms afraid to move her. I told her how much I loved her and how brave she was. I assured her she would make it and all would be fine. The ambulance arrived and we went to the hospital.

I had waited with Samantha, never leaving her side, except for when they did the tests that showed why she was in a coma.

She had swelling where he hit her. I prayed. I had held her hand; I never left her.

I begged God, "Please God, please...I promise you anything."

Mom, my brother and Gram showed up the night before. Miranda had left a note on my door and steered them to the hospital. They came in and sat with me, Gram never far away. They were my source of support. All the problems that had ensued the years before...they were gone. We were a family again.

It was now a few days later and I sat here in the chapel of the hospital, exhausted. For the last 78 hours, she just lay there, unable to speak, unable to hear possibly. I had spoken to her in hopes of her hearing me. I had told her of my love for her. I laid with her, prayed with her hand in mine.

She couldn't die, "Please, Please don't let her die," I muttered. My eyes looked towards the heavens as I prayed with every piece of energy I had left. I hadn't slept in three days. I prayed so long and hard that I finally fell into a deep sleep.

In my sleep I dreamt I was standing on the banks of the lake...looking out over the water...beckoning her to come. Please come help me again. Please come to me angel I need your help. Where are you?

I shielded my eyes from the glaring sun; looking out over the water. Was that her? She was walking towards me. I felt relief, she would help me. Walk faster I thought as she took solid steps towards me. I wanted to run to her, but the water stopped me. As I stepped into the water, my feet were wet. I wasn't walking on the water as she had. I had to wait. Tears stained my clothing as I wept for her coming to me. She would help me. She would help. She was nearing. I covered my eyes with my hands, weeping mournfully again. As she arrived I took my hands from my eyes, she had features this time. It was Samantha.

Chapter Seventeen

I awoke screaming. "Oh my God...It was Samantha. She was Sam."

I ran from the chapel, down the hall to her room. If she was my angel, and my angel had features, then she was dead. I wanted to scream in terror. What would I do now? I moved past Gram, fluid motion and threw myself on the bed. I grabbed Samantha and held her. I was sobbing uncontrollably.

I just kept saying, "Samantha, Samantha. Samantha..." I sobbed. She couldn't be dead. She just couldn't be.

That familiar hand patted my head. I wanted it to go away. Not now, my auburn angel couldn't help now. I was going to will myself to die with her.

"Go away..." I screamed. I didn't need her; I needed Samantha. I hadn't ever told her I loved her to her face, while she was awake.

I began saying it, "I love you, Samantha. I love you. I should have told you. I should have told you. I love you so much, why did you have to die? Why? Why?"

I was still sobbing out of control. The hand patted me lightly again. It was stroking my hair.

"Abby, I heard you the night at Gram's." She said.

I was sobbing so loud that I thought I had misunderstood the auburn angel. I pulled myself off Samantha's chest. It wasn't the auburn angel. It was Samantha patting my head. She wasn't dead. She was talking to me.

I kissed her face all over, careful not to hurt her. "Oh my God, I thought you were dead. I had a dream you were her, she was you," I stammered. "I was in the chapel and I thought when

I saw it was her...or you were her...or whatever, that you were dead and you were my angel now. It's you, baby, it's you."

She grimaced in pain and her other hand went to her head. "What happened? All I remember is he was going to kill her..." she looked at me.

"Oh baby, don't worry about it. I'll tell you about it later. It's okay. Everyone is okay, Baby. We were worried about you." I said.

She looked at me again. "My head hurts, Abby." Her voice was incredibly hoarse.

The nurse entered at that time and pressed the button on Sam's bed. Two other nurses came in and began examining her and one left to get the doctor. The doctor came in and pronounced that Samantha was going to have a headache for a few months probably, but that they tests had shown no implications of real damage, they were more worried about her waking from the coma.

He patted my back and I hugged him. "I think she is going to be fine. I'll order tests immediately, just to make sure. But, this is a good sign." He was smiling.

Gram walked to me and put her arms around me and said, "Sweet Samantha, you gave this poor child quite a scare. She hasn't left your side in three days. You were in the coma and she was beside herself. She won't eat and she won't sleep. I gave her something the other day and asked her to give it to you and do something for me. It was a bit selfish on my part, but I think this is as good a time as any for her to do it."

I caught on real quick as Gram spoke and reached in my pocket. I hadn't changed clothing since we had arrived. The ring was still in my pocket. I took it in my hand, the ring box, and sat on the bed. I took Samantha's hand in mine and said, "Samantha, you are more than an angel to me. I love you more than I have words to express. Because of this, I would like for you to have this," as I opened the ring box, I spoke. My words continuing as Samantha looked in the ring box. "Will you make a life with me forever Samantha? Will you marry me?"

She let me place the ring on her hand, as she gazed into my eyes "Yes Abby, I would like nothing more."

❧

We were married Dec. 27th and left for the Bahamas on Dec. 28th for Samantha's birthday present. She had come out of the hospital and not had much of a problem, only headaches that didn't go away for three weeks. Gram stayed with us, while I worked, and took care of Sam. She wouldn't be leaving until we returned from the Bahamas; she was more worried about Samantha than even I was. Sam couldn't do anything for herself with the "matron" around, as Gram referred to herself.

I had finished planning the fund-raiser for the shelter and it had been a huge success. After the accident, the community supported the shelter even more. They had done a full-page story on Samantha, Miranda and myself and told everyone what bravery we had shown in the crisis. Because of it, we had to sell the current shelter and purchase new ones though; the confidentiality had been blown. I took care of everything because Samantha wasn't allowed to work yet.

Our vacation in the Bahamas was the last part of her recovery. When we got back, she would return to work and spend the $1.67 million dollars I had raised for her to make her dreams come alive.